P9-DFI-276

THIS
WAS
THE
NORTH

THIS WAS THE NORTH

BY ANTON MONEY
WITH BEN EAST

CROWN PUBLISHERS, INC., NEW YORK

Gardner-Webb College Library

All quotations at chapter openings
are from poems by Robert Service, from
The Collected Poems of Robert Service.
Reprinted by permission of Dodd, Mead
& Company, and McGraw-Hill Ryerson Limited.

This Was the North is based in part on articles
by Anton Money that originally appeared in the
June, July, August, and September 1972 issues of
Outdoor Life magazine, © 1972 by Popular Science
Publishing Company, Inc. Used by permission.

© 1975 by Anton Money and Ben East
All rights reserved. No part of this book
may be reproduced or utilized in any form or by any
means, electronic or mechanical, including
photocopying, recording, or by any information
storage and retrieval system, without permission
in writing from the publisher. Inquiries should
be addressed to Crown Publishers, Inc., 419 Park
Avenue South, New York, N.Y. 10016

Manufactured in the United States of America
Published simultaneously in Canada by
General Publishing Company Limited

Library of Congress Cataloging in Publication Data

Money, Anton.
    This was the north.

        1.   Frances Lake region, Yukon Territory—Gold discoveries.
2.   Money, Anton.   I.   East, Ben, joint author.
II.   Title.
F1095.F7M65   917.19'1'0430924   75-9997
ISBN 0-517-51892-9

Second Printing, September, 1975

F
1095
F7
m65

To the men
with whom I shared
the rapids and the trail

THIS WAS THE NORTH is Anton Money's story. He lived it, wrote the first draft of his experiences, and then added passages after his collaborator had put his material into professional form. I have tried to retain as much of the original flavor as possible—which at times includes images and passages that mean much to the man who lived the story.

THE EDITOR

CONTENTS

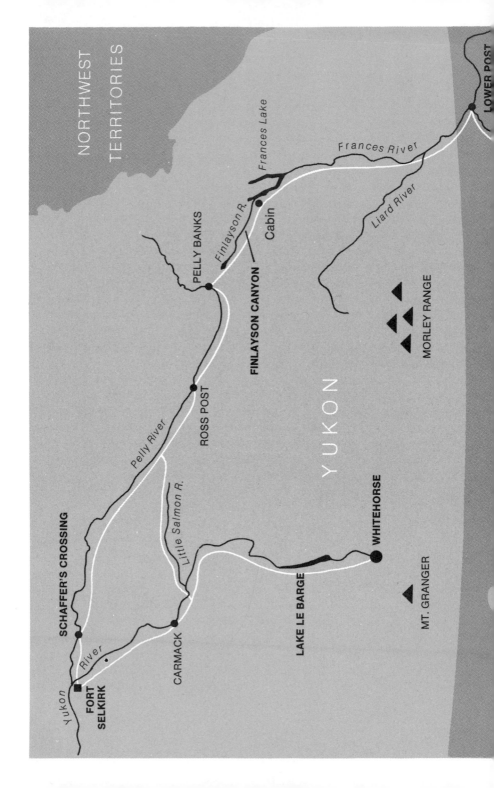

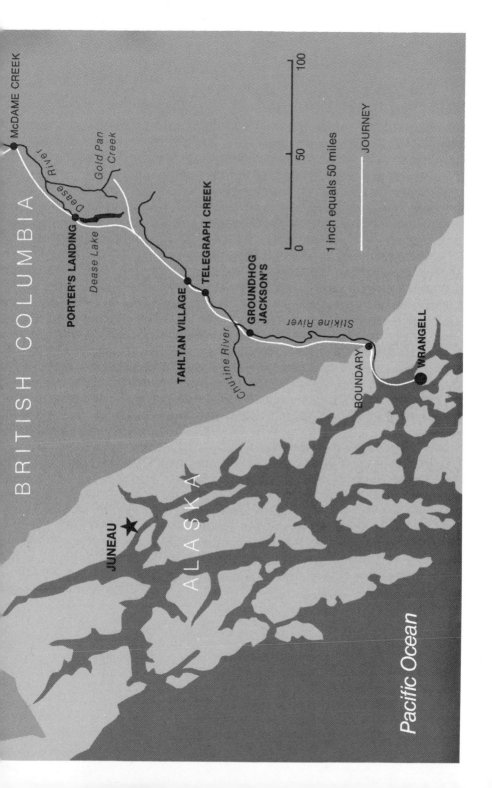

THIS
WAS
THE
NORTH

1
TELEGRAPH CREEK

I'm sick to death of your well-groomed gods, your
make-believe and your show,
I long for a whiff of bacon and beans, a snug shake-
down in the snow.
—*"The Heart of the Sourdough"*

At noon on a sunny day in late May of 1923, when the northern earth was vibrant with awakening life, the *Hazel B No. 2*, a shallow-draft riverboat drawing only two feet of water, nosed into the bank at Telegraph Creek, 165 miles up the Stikine River from salt water at Wrangell.

Deaf Dan, our pilot, and Dar Smith, purser and deck-hand, jumped ashore and made the bow and stern lines fast to two big cottonwoods where a roadway led down to the beach. There was no dock at Telegraph Creek. Captain Syd Barrington, our skipper, called for a gangplank to be put out, and Jack, the cook, stepped to the rail and started tossing scraps to a dozen gaunt and hungry sled dogs that lined the beach. It had taken us three long days to come up the river against the tumbling, knifing, snow-fed current of the Stikine. The *Hazel B* would make the return run downstream in ten hours.

Of the twenty-odd passengers, Indian and white, aboard the riverboat I was the only one to whom the country was entirely new, and I thrilled in the excitement and color of the scene before me. Telegraph Creek occupied the banks

1

either side of the creek by the same name. The creek had cut an amphitheatre in the sheer lava rock walls just large enough to hold the little town. Behind the town loomed high timber-covered mountains. The town had gained its name many years before when the telegraph line going north crossed the river at that point. Two rows of houses faced the river, and a schoolhouse, government office, the Hudson's Bay Company post, and a couple of outfitters' places made up Telegraph Creek; it sheltered twenty white residents and some two hundred Indians. The town was the jumping-off place for the great Cassiar Mining District, covering an area of more than seventy thousand square miles. A few buildings were of lumber, dressed and painted, but more were of logs, some of them hewed square, notched and fitted at the corners, and snugly chinked. Some of the roofs were shingle, others corrugated metal.

Ours was the first boat to come up from tidewater since the previous October. All through the winter the remote little outpost had been cut off from the outside world. There was no radio at that time, and the winter isolation was complete. Our arrival meant the renewal of contact, the beginning of the summer rush. From now until freeze-up a weekly boat would come churning up the Stikine, bringing a handful of passengers and a load of supplies and equipment. Prospectors and, later on, hunting parties would outfit here, pack trains would leave for trading posts in the interior. New men would be coming into the country, and for the younger women at Telegraph Creek, that meant new interests and fun.

For everybody there, white and Indian alike, this day when the first boat of the year arrived was the Great Day of the year. It meant mail, fresh foods not known since the last boat had followed the slush ice down the river the previous autumn. It meant Indian trappers coming home from their traplines with the winter's catch, old-timers greeting one another after a separation perhaps of years, with shouts of warm but derisive welcome bandied back and forth across the water as the *Hazel B* nudged toward the bank.

All of Telegraph Creek had turned out to welcome us. Young and old alike, they lined the edge of the main street overlooking the river from the top of the bank thirty feet above. The few white women were dressed in spring cottons, the men mostly in khaki overalls. Alongside the finery of the Indians, the multicolored head scarves, the beaded jackets and moccasins, the purple, yellow and blue blouses and dresses, the white cotton clothing actually looked drab.

A few men came aboard to greet Captain Barrington and the crew. The passengers carried their gear down the gangplank and up the steep bank to the street. Mail went ashore and was quickly packed off to the Hudson's Bay Company store for distribution.

Two independent traders, Frank Callbreath and Bob Hyland, had left their trading posts to stand with Harry Dodd, the gold commissioner, watching the bustle. The Reverend Thorman and his English bride joined Jackson, the telegraph operator, and his wife, greeted old friends, as did Scott Simpson, Indian agent of forty years' standing, whom I would come to know as the Grand Old Man of the Cassiar.

It was like the beginning of a summer fair, I told myself. Telegraph Creek would boom now for five months— until snow fell again and the river froze, and the isolation of winter settled over the place once more.

This was the North, Robert Service's land of abysmal loneliness, vast and untamed and beautiful, stretching away into endless distances of mountain and valley, river and lake, with places of solitude where no human had walked. Men spoke of traveling the rivers for days or even weeks on end without encountering another person. How strange that seemed to one accustomed to the short distances of Europe, where a journey of a few hundred miles could take you out of one country, across a second, and into a third.

This sprawling land was the country of dreams to which I had come from a third of the way around the world. It was also the frontier, raw and harsh, seductive and brutal by turn. It would have been hard to imagine any place on earth more completely unlike the pastoral, long-settled countryside in the south of England, where except for war service I had spent all the twenty-two years of my life.

It was on this northern frontier, this wilderness of miners and trappers, Indians and whites, brawling rivers and silent valleys, that I intended to make a place for myself. It was also here, in the peace and quiet of a magnificent land almost unpeopled, that I hoped to escape the pressures of the so-called civilized world, pressures that even in 1923 were becoming more than I chose to endure.

I was not, as today's generation says, copping out. I was seeking a place where I could make my own way by whatever ability I had, where values were honest and genuine, where life itself depended on a man's own resourcefulness and resolution, where the laws that ruled were inexorable because they were natural laws. Somehow, at twenty-two I preferred that to the man-made rules and dubious values I had known in England.

But mostly, I had come here because, without even having seen it, I was in love with this immense, beautiful, siren land called the North.

The superstitious would say I began life under a lucky star. I was born on September 16, 1900, on a country estate near the village of Albury in Surrey, not far from London, one of eleven children and the seventh son of a seventh son. You can hardly inherit more potent magic than that, and in the new land I had chosen I would need it all.

Ours was a fine old home that dated back to the tenth century, and it was a pleasant place in which to grow up. I still recall the happy days of childhood with my brothers and a younger sister, the tennis and croquet parties all summer long, the call for tea when we had to change our clothes and wear a blazer and be tidy and proper. I can still see the great old tulip tree beneath which tea was served in fine weather, the silver kettle on its swinging stand, the tiny bread-and-butter sandwiches we were required to eat before we could take cakes.

I remember well the sedate walks we had with our Scottish nurse through the beech woods on the huge estate of our neighbor, the Duke of Northumberland, and how we went through farms and across a bridge over the Tilling-bourne River to get there. I also remember how Madge-wick, our coachman and head gardener, used to chase us out of the kitchen garden when we tried to swipe green apples or plums, and how the upstairs maid Yeldom brought us our morning tea and biscuits in bed. Ah, the grand pillow fights we had!

It was a happy growing up. Later there was school at Cranleigh, a typical English public school, with two older brothers. My other older brothers were in the Colonies by the time I started school. My years in school were in no way unusual. We had soccer and cricket games, gym and rifle teams, and long cross-country runs that took us across farm fields, through cool woods where the bracken was deep and damp, over commons covered with heather and gorse. I got onto the running and gym teams, and later the rifle team.

Then came World War I, and the happy days were over. Before the war ended, it had claimed all of my brothers. The older ones came home to England to join the army and die. I lost one each year from 1914 through 1918, another in Persia soon after as a result of the war, and in the end the seventh son was the only one left.

I had had five years of officers' training at school. I joined up in 1917, a bit under age, and served two years. I drew a billet as an instructor and escaped the mud and cold and horror of the trenches, but, still, when the fighting stopped and those of us who were left were back in Eng-land, I was a different man.

I had joined with a flag in one hand and a gun in the other, fighting mad and burning to take revenge on the ene-mies of England. Now I found myself disillusioned and bitter, wondering at the wrongs, the stupidities, the greed and the waste, and most of all at the loss of young men like my own brothers, whose lives were just beginning. It was in part that reaction, I think, that would drive me a third of the way around the globe, to a new home in the wilderness of the North.

My father had been a government mining engineer and, although he had retired early in the war, engineers and explorers from the farthest corners of the earth continued to be frequent visitors in our home. Often they stayed for a week at a time, and I listened openmouthed to the marvelous tales they had to tell. Slowly an unquenchable desire began to take shape in my mind. The faraway Lorelei North was starting to wrap her arms around me. I read the books of Jack London and the poems of Robert Service, anything I could find on that distant and romantic land. I crammed at mining engineering with a private tutor after my release from the service, but my heart was not in it.

I had good offers from uncles and cousins, to plant rubber in Ceylon or tea in Darjeeling, but these held no appeal. Those were not the places I wanted to go to, and that was not the life I wanted to lead. I ached for the challenges and solitude of a harsher land, a land where I could stand on my own and succeed or fail with no influence and no help from family or home.

Finally I applied for and got a job as a clerk with the Hudson's Bay Company, the romance-freighted "Company of Adventurers of England" that had traded in the North since 1670. I arranged to serve at one of the northwest posts.

I reached Vancouver in early May that spring of 1923, and booked passage north to Wrangell on the Canadian Pacific S.S. *Princess Alice*. We plodded our way north along the coast of British Columbia, through the breathtaking beauty of the Inside Passage, for three days, and in one sense the voyage was a disillusionment. Most of the passengers were men who had lived for many years in this northland—miners, prospectors, traders, fur buyers. It was clear they did not share my greenhorn's enthusiasm and sense of adventure. For the most part they stayed in the lounges and played poker, while I paced the deck in a heavy overcoat to watch the scenery. It was hard then for me to understand how anyone could ever grow blasé about such country.

I stepped off the *Princess Alice* onto Alaskan soil with a dozen or so other men, and we headed in a band for Wrangell's only hotel. It was clean but primitive, and I was assigned to a room with another guest. He was a grizzled, weathered character of about forty-five and he thrust out a hand as hard as a steel vise.

"My name's Amos Godfrey," he introduced himself. "Guess we'll be sharin' this room until the first boat goes upriver."

If my voyage north from Vancouver had been something of a disappointment, my week's stay in Wrangell more than made up for it. The town fascinated me, with its totem poles, its false-front wooden stores, its curio shops, Indians living it up in noisy cafés, the mountains that frowned down on it, the fishing boats, and the smell of the sea. And the lobby of the hotel bustled all day long with reminders of the wilderness that shut Wrangell in. The first day I was there two trappers came in from their winter trapping grounds on the British Columbia–Alaska border, unloaded their canoe, and piled their catch of beaver pelts high on the lobby floor. I watched big-eyed as a local fur buyer sorted and graded the round dry skins with their lustrous deep fur.

Before the job was finished, another trapper came in with a fabulous assortment of pelts and the lobby buzzed with talk of fur prices and catches.

I struck up a conversation with the newcomer and learned that his name was Jim Lovett. "Them two'll clean up about forty-five hundred dollars," he confided, nodding toward the trapper team.

I whistled. So this was how men made fortunes in this remote land. Forty-five hundred dollars for hardly more than two months of hard and lonely work. I recalled what the owner of a curio shop had said when I told him I was going up to Telegraph Creek to work for the Hudson's Bay Company. He had leaned his elbows on the counter and eyed me with an amused grin. "Plenty of young fellows start out that way, but the creeks get to pulling at them and the first thing they know they're off digging for gold or trapping for furs."

Likely he was right. I itched for a load of traps and a canoe and a trapline of my own. And my excitement and

The harbor and city of Wrangell, Alaska, 1923.

Main Street, Wrangell, 1923.

enthusiasm mounted even higher when Jim Lovett un-
wrapped his bundle of mink and marten, otter and fox pelts,
the most silky and beautiful things I had ever touched.

He trapped, he said, up the Iskoot, a tributary of the
Stikine just above the British Columbia border. In the summer he prospected and worked a small mining claim. He
made it sound easy, and I was more sure than ever that I
had chosen the right life.

The day came finally when the *Hazel B No. 2*, one of
a fleet of four riverboats operated by Captain Barrington,
all named *Hazel B* after his wife and numbered from one
to four, was ready for the year's first run up the Stikine.

2
THE CHEECHAKO

Have you gazed on naked grandeur where there's
nothing else to gaze on,
Set pieces and drop-curtain scenes galore,
Big mountains heaved to heaven, which the blinding
sunsets blazon,
Black canyons where the rapids rip and roar?
—"The Call of the Wild"

Twenty of us loaded our baggage and trappings aboard the *Hazel B.* All except me were old hands in the country, miners, trappers or men with jobs of one sort or another back in the mountains. Within a few minutes I had met Dar Smith, the purser and general deckhand; the engineer who nursed the twin 250-horsepower diesel engines; Deaf Dan, the pilot; and Jack the cook. Last of all I met Captain Barrington, veteran of Alaskan rivers, tall and lean, tanned by sun and wind, who studied me with clear keen eyes, chewing on a long cigar as he welcomed me aboard.

Our departure was keyed to the rising tide to enable the *Hazel B* to clear the sandbars at the mouth of the Stikine. We eased away from the dock and headed out across the seven miles of salt water that lay between Wrangell and the river, rolling and wallowing despite the shelter of the mountainous islands that enclosed the Inside Passage. We turned into the Stikine, between the wide mud flats of the delta, shortly before suppertime, putting up a raft of hundreds of ducks that circled the boat like a swarm of locusts. A wind was blasting downriver, carrying the chill of the snow and glaciers up in the high peaks. Enchanted as I was with every yard of the trip, I sought shelter in the small lounge below the pilothouse.

Amos, my roommate from the hotel at Wrangell, was there, arguing loudly with another miner about claims, while others compared notes or swapped lies about their gold digging. Many had no claims but were going into the wilderness to prospect, spurred by the eternal will-o'-the-wisp of making a rich strike. The talk centered on one of the older men who had just made a new strike on McDame Creek, where seven million dollars in gold had been recovered during the 1870s. Almost without exception, to judge by the tales they told, these tough, hardened men with a stubble of beard on their chins had come within a hair's breadth of wealth, and often it was some accident of nature that had cheated them of their big chance.

"The damn water dried up on me in August," one grizzled character complained. "If she'd kept flowin' one more month I'd a'had the bedrock cleaned off clear down to China Bar. Now I got that job to do all over again." He slumped in his chair and stretched his legs out, bone weary at the very thought. But then his eyes lit up and he sat forward again in a hurry as a newcomer joined the group.

This one had a bottle of rum in his hand and he proceeded to pass it around. Each man took a swig from the bottle in turn, something I had never seen done before. I was fourth or fifth in line and it was passed to me as a matter of course. I gulped down my swig and it took my breath away and hit my belly like liquid fire. I resisted the desire to cough or wipe away tears, but it was five minutes before I could speak again.

The supper bell saved me. It sounded, and Jack the cook called from his tiny galley, "Come and get it!"

I had come for adventure and excitement and almost every bend of the Stikine supplied them. The river entered the mountains while we were at supper that first evening. We rounded a wide-sweeping curve, and suddenly we were cut off, imprisoned in a world of our own, unlike any I had ever seen. The mountains tumbled steeply to the water's edge and the powerful diesels sent a rumbling echo back from the granite walls on both sides, like the growl of thunder. The river ran between those confining walls in a narrow smooth ribbon and the captain held the boat to the middle of it. The engines throbbed and hammered and the *Hazel B* clawed her way steadily against the millrace of the current.

Ahead, beyond the nearer mountains, snow peaks shone in the westering sun, and in the high valleys glaciers lay like frozen rivers with ruffled surfaces, turned motionless as they crawled toward the Stikine. Waterfalls cascaded down cliffs of bare rock, falling hundreds of feet, to be lost in the timber and brush of the valley floor. Those falling waters were carrying millions of tons of snow, melting now in the warmth of May, down from the mountains to swell the river on its way to the sea. The late sun cast lights and shadows of every possible hue over the whole wild scene, and in the valleys the young green of poplar and willow stood in bright contrast to the somber darkness of fir and spruce.

Nothing I had seen in England had prepared me for the beauty and vastness of these mountains. It has been more than fifty years since I stood on the deck of that riverboat

The *Hazel B No. 2* on the Stikine.

but the loveliness and majesty is as fresh in my mind today as it was on that long-ago evening.

Smitty, the deckhand, came up from supper and Captain Barrington called to him, "Give me the mark."

Smitty picked up a fifteen-foot pole, the lower six feet of which was marked off in foot lengths painted alternate colors. He plunged the tip of it to the river bottom and called out "Four feet." He tested again. "Three feet." The skipper changed the heading slightly and the next sounding showed "Three six." That went on for half an hour, until we were past the treacherous stretch of shallow river, with the *Hazel B* changing course repeatedly, swinging back and forth across the current to keep to the deepest part of the channel. The skill needed by a riverboat captain on the Stikine was hard to believe.

Before darkness settled over the river, we tied up at the Customs and Immigration House on the boundary between Alaska and British Columbia. The business of clearing customs took only a short time; because we were the first boat of the year, the customs officer had come upriver with us.

One other scene from that trip is etched unforgettably in my memory. While we were tied up for the night at the Customs House, in the purple velvet dusk of the valley, with the high peaks still gilded by the last rays of the sun, the cook came out on deck and began playing soft airs on a concertina. The melodies were gentle at first, the old songs of yesteryear, seeming to keep time with the whisper of water around the bow of the boat. One by one the men came from their staterooms or the lounge, squatting on the deck or standing in a silent circle. Then, hesitantly at first, the singing began.

They were a rough crew, those miners and trappers, hard-cursing men, but for a moment, held in a gentle bondage by the music and the peace and silence that lay over the wild Stikine, I suspect each one of them was touched with longing for some faraway home that he would not likely see again.

It was Jack who broke the spell of that northern night. He changed the tempo of his playing, and the songs changed

with it; they became rollicking and lusty. The men sang of
the stampede, of the river, of mountain and lass, of old
Kentucky and Scotland. A big Swede launched into a song
of his own country in his own tongue, and Jack caught the
tune and followed him as if he had known it always.

That was one evening of my life that I shall remember
to the last day. It was full dark when we went to our bunks,
although light still lingered on the high snowfields, and even
then I was too full of emotion begotten by that sweet and
lonely music to want to sleep.

I tumbled out at the first streaks of dawn, not wanting
to miss anything, and as I rounded the corner of the deck-
house I was made welcome to the fraternity of this wild
land.

Jack the cook poked his grinning face out of the galley
and held out a huge steaming cup. "Coffee, cheechako?"

He had used the word of Alaska and all the Northwest
for greenhorn. Cheechako. And I welcomed it. Cheechako
I was, a tenderfoot fresh out from England, but the very
application of that term and the friendly tone with which
it was used told me that I had taken the first step toward
being accepted by the breed of rough men I had come to
live among. I was proud to be called by it. In time I would
earn the right to discard it. Meanwhile I'd make the most of
the friendliness it implied.

Before the last of us had finished breakfast that morning, we reached the Great Glacier. A mass of ice five miles
wide and five hundred feet thick crept slowly down from
a permanent ice field at the crest of the mountains that lay
on the Alaska–British Columbia boundary. Curving and
twisting around sheer walls of bare rock, the huge river of
ice came to rest now, melting as fast as it advanced, two
miles back from the Stikine. Once, legend had it, it had
scoured its way entirely across the valley and the river had
flowed through a tunnel under the ice. I would hear that
story again before the summer was over, from the lips of a
wrinkled Indian, old Casca John, on the Tahltan River
farther back in the mountains, and it would be one of the
strangest tales I listened to in all my years in that country.

Now, in curious contrast to the mighty ice river, a hot spring bubbled out of the ground close to the bank of the Stikine, its steam a ghostly plume in the light of early morning. Higher up, the rising sun was touching the glacier, turning it to a winding spangled ribbon of jewels.

In midmorning, just below the mouth of the Skud River, we came to the swiftest current we had yet encountered. Watching the bank, it was difficult to tell if the *Hazel B* was making any headway at all. Captain Barrington fought a long battle with the tumbling water, but finally he put the bow of the boat aground on a gravel bar. There was a call for volunteers. Deaf Dan, with half a dozen passengers including me, jumped ashore. We grabbed the end of a steel cable and dragged it up the beach to the head of the fast water. There we made it fast to two big trees and Deaf Dan signaled the skipper. The boat backed off the gravel bar, swung out into the current, and began to move upstream. It was being winched by the slow but inexorable power of that cable, wound around the capstan. Above the rapids Captain Syd headed into shore and picked us up.

For the first twenty or thirty miles above the sea, the tide had made itself felt in the Stikine and we had had a great deal of slack water. But now, in the upper river above the Skud, it turned fast and wild, twisting and coiling down its rocky channel like a living thing, running at millrace speed even between rapids—"riffles," the rivermen called them, but that seemed an inadequate word for those plunging reaches, where time after time the current was too much for the powerful engines of the *Hazel B* and we had to resort to lining. Half a dozen crew members and volunteers would jump ashore at the foot of the rapids. I made it a point to help at every opportunity, in part because I counted it fun, in part because it struck me as part of my education in the North. Sometimes we could do the lining by hand, without resorting to the steel cable and capstan.

Just before dark the second day we tied up for the night not far below a stretch known as the canyon, where the river plunged a full mile between sheer granite walls. The passengers and crew went ashore and built up a huge

Passengers lining the *Hazel B* around a rapids on an early spring run up the Stikine.

fire of blazing logs. They gathered around it in a circle, and soon the singing started again, lusty voices ringing out loud and clear in the stillness of the wilderness night, men glorying in their freedom. I walked a short distance up the beach to look back at the scene. The fire sent its sparks into the darkness and the figures ringed the bright area; I could see the dark shape of the *Hazel B* tied at the shore with its lighted windows shining out across the black river. It was one more scene etched indelibly in my memory.

The highlight of the trip for me came shortly after we started on the next morning, as we approached the canyon. Captain Barrington caught my eye from the pilothouse and called to me, "Come on up for a spell." That was good fortune beyond my fondest dreams. An invitation to the pilothouse, the holy of holies on any boat, was something I had not even hoped for. My help at lining must be paying off, I told myself as I clambered up the ladder. I know now it was more than that. It was a kindly river captain giving a young greenhorn something to go on.

"You seem to be doing all right for a young cheechako," the skipper greeted me. Then, after a pause, "So you're going to work for the HBC. Well, it wouldn't surprise me any if you go out soon with one of the mining companies."

It was the second time a prediction of that kind had been made, and I was beginning to feel that the forecasts were accurate.

There was a silence while the captain and I shared the pilothouse windows facing upstream, watching the swirls of water go careering past. Every now and then I glanced at his powerful hands on the wheel and wondered what the feel of steering the boat against the tumbling current would be like. And then, suddenly and totally unexpectedly, Captain Syd offered: "Hold her while I light another smoke."

I wrapped my hands around the spokes and felt the stabbing rush of the river come up through the wheel. Smitty appeared on deck and the captain called for two coffees. The deckhand brought them up to the pilothouse, and his jaw dropped when he saw who was at the wheel. "Got a new pilot," Captain Syd chuckled. I felt enormously proud. "Might as well make him useful. Think I'll teach him to take us through the canyon."

His gruff joking gave me a warm and wonderful feeling. Back in Vancouver I had been afraid that in the North I'd find myself an unwanted stranger, a tenderfoot Englishman shunned and snubbed. Now, however much kidding I might take for my lack of knowledge, I was already being accepted as if I belonged.

We rounded a bend and the canyon came in sight. The captain shouldered me aside, took the wheel again, and the *Hazel B* drove in between the granite cliffs, bucking a current so swift that the river was piled higher in midstream than along the sides. Captain Barrington fell back on a strange technique to best it. He'd let the current catch the bow of the boat and as it swung he'd use the full power of the engines to claw diagonally toward one rock wall. At the last instant he'd swing toward the opposite side, like a ship tacking under sail, with the current taking the place of the wind. It called for keen judgment and split-second timing, but each time we tacked we gained a few feet upstream. The passengers crowded the deck to watch, heedless of the water that foamed against the bow and the spray that drenched them.

Finally we broke out of the head of the canyon: it was as if we had entered another world.

Up to now the mountains that had hemmed us in had been steep towering ramparts with snow peaks, and ice in the high valleys; ahead they were low and rounded, timbered or grass grown. The river slowed and the high banks gave way to flat benches cloaked with parklike stands of poplar and pine. There was almost no underbrush, no moss on the trees, and the tangles of devil's club that had fringed the downstream banks were gone.

I was still in the pilothouse and I could look out over the tops of a grove of aspens on a bench beside the river. They looked as level and even as if they had been sheared, and I asked Captain Syd about it.

"That's the rabbits," he told me solemnly. "When the snow gets deep they eat the tops off the trees and that leaves 'em all the same height."

I stared at the twenty-foot aspens, too green to know whether to believe him. But when I looked at him again there was a telltale twinkle in his eyes. I was sure then that I had been accepted, but I also realized that a cheechako is easily taken in.

Here in these gentler mountains, a miner's cabin stood at the mouth of almost every creek, low roofed and snug, with log walls and sod roof. Beside each cabin a small cache on poles provided safe storage from bears, wolves, or wolverines.

At a few of the cabins we pulled in to the bank and tied up briefly, to leave mail or supplies.

There was one where a very old man stood on the bank and watched us approach, with a shaggy-coated, ancient horse resting its head on his shoulder as if leaning on him. "Not sure which is older, that horse or Old Man Kirk," Captain Syd chuckled.

There was another where a full-grown cow moose stood within arm's length of the owner of the place. Rescued as a calf and raised as a pet, she followed her owner around like a dog.

At dark the third night we tied up at the ghost town of

Glenora. There had been a trading post there as far back as the 1870s, but it was not until the stampede to the Klondike in '98 that Glenora grew overnight into a bustling and brawling outpost. It was then the head of navigation on the Stikine, on the way to Dawson City, and more than 10,000 people had wintered there that year. Of that number hardly more than a handful ever made it through to Dawson. The old graveyard told what happened to many of them. Others stayed on to rediscover and work the fabulously rich creeks of Dease Lake, McDame Creek, and the tributaries of the upper Liard, notably Sayyea Creek, hundreds of miles back in the interior.

In 1923 a few of the old buildings had fallen down, but most were standing and intact, having withstood the rigors of weather and the heavy snows of winter for twenty-five years. The stout log jail at one end of the main street, with its barred windows, still spoke mutely of gold-camp life. The Northwest Mounted Police had kept order in '98, and the jail had never wanted for occupants. By the time I saw the place, the head of navigation had moved twelve miles up the Stikine to Telegraph Creek. Today nothing remains of Glenora except a few headstones in the cemetery.

Of all the tales I had heard since I arrived in Wrangell, the one that fascinated me most—and still does, down to the present day—was told that night by Captain Conover, an old-time trapper and prospector on the Clearwater, who had come aboard the *Hazel B* at the mouth of that river to travel with us to Telegraph Creek. Working fifteen or twenty miles up the Clearwater, he said, he had found a crevice cutting across the bedrock of the stream. At extremely low water he had managed to get at the exposed edges of that crevice, and inching into it he had found a fabulous deposit of gold nuggets. Then rising water had "drowned him out."

"She's there," the old man insisted. "Richest strike I've ever seen. I'll get her this year if I have to lift the whole damned river over my head in a box!"

I could see skepticism on the faces of many of his listeners, but it seemed to me that it was not because they disbelieved his story but rather because they doubted that

The Stikine Hotel
in Telegraph Creek.

he could ever work the gold he had found. So far as I know, neither the old trapper nor anyone else ever got into that crevice. Does a fortune in gold still lie bedded there, under the swift current of the Clearwater, a fabled El Dorado waiting for someone to rediscover and recover it? Who can say?

It was noon when we came in sight of the town of Telegraph Creek. The most exciting journey of my life up to that time was finished.

I carried my gear up to the Hudson's Bay Company store and introduced myself to John Boyd, the factor. My first look at him recalled what Amos Godfrey, my roommate in the hotel at Wrangell, had said when I told him where I was to work.

"Johnny Boyd?" Godfrey had grunted. "That old goat has been there since before I come up here prospecting. He's that thin and palelike, the Indians call him Nodan. Means The Ghost."

Boyd was indeed thin and pale enough to qualify. He passed me over to Jimmy Lowe, a young assistant my own age, a year out from Scotland. Jimmy led me to a dingy room in the Hudson's Bay Hotel. Then he took me in tow to show me the town.

I was beginning, that May afternoon, forty eventful and adventure-filled years ago, years that would take me into the outermost corners of this huge northern wilderness. I would pan for gold, learn to drive a dog team, whipsaw my own lumber for a cabin, live with Indians who had never seen a white man before, and relish the stillness and solitude of winter when there was no other human within a hundred miles of me.

Long before those forty years were up the cheechako would be a full-fledged sourdough, ready for any challenge the North held out. I would find the gold that lured me, and I would also find a boundless love for the wild and cruel but beautiful land, a love that will endure as long as I live.

3

THE EAGLE FEATHER

The Arctic trails have their secret tales
That would make your blood run cold.
— "The Cremation of Sam McGee"

I entered into my new job with the zest of a pilgrim who has arrived at the holy city.

Jimmy Lowe, to whom Boyd had handed me over, turned out to be a good companion. He had never been outside his native city of Glasgow until the Company had recruited him for a life at its trading posts and he had come out to Canada as an apprentice on a five-year contract. He was paid almost nothing, but the company gave him room and board, such as it was. He lived in one room at the old rundown company hotel. It burned later, never to be rebuilt.

I had been hired at a better salary than Jimmy's and was more fortunate in my housing. Boyd, the factor, had a small bungalow on a hill that looked across the river to the mountains on the far side. Because he preferred living in rooms over the trading post, he put me up in the bungalow. These were pleasant quarters and I learned to cook my own meals, often with Jimmy's help.

Weekends he and I hiked out and saw as much of the surrounding country as we could, camping overnight wherever we fancied, catching fish for our meals, making bannock, mastering the fundamentals of wilderness living.

The most fascinating part of my work was trading with the Indians. Their trapping season wound up in May with the annual spring beaver hunt. By the beginning of June even those whose traplines were farthest from Telegraph Creek were showing up at the trading post, pitching their tents along the high bank across the river from the town. By the time the short arctic summer set in, with its long days of sunshine and nights of no real darkness, there were some three hundred Indians camped in the area.

Hunting was good, and moose and caribou and wild sheep meat simmered in big smoke-blackened kettles all day long and far into the night. Children with ragged clothing and dirty faces ran in and out of the tents at will, never scolded. And tied to nearby trees, out of one another's reach, were the sled dogs that were then a part of every Indian

Jimmy Lowe, a Hudson's Bay Company apprentice and my companion in my first adventures in Alaska. While I worked for H.B.C. I lived in the cottage at upper left.

camp in the North, gaunt, half-starved animals, equally ready to fight, pilfer food or break into the wild and savage howling that was, next to the wolf howl—which I have always thought a beautiful song, with its ascending and slowly descending half tones—the loneliest and most blood-chilling sound I have ever listened to. There were at least as many dogs as humans in the Indian camp, and when a hundred or more of them howled in unison, it was a chorus no one would ever forget.

Those sled dogs became a way of life. They were always hungry, for the Indians did not believe in feeding a dog unless he was earning his keep. Many of them had some wolf blood and they were almost as wild and fierce as wolves.

For the Indians this was the fun season. Since the previous October they had worked hard on their far-flung traplines, usually one family in a place. Now they had come to the trading posts to barter their pelts for supplies and the few knickknacks that appealed to them, and to enjoy the year's only social life. Always they tried to get rid of their poorest skins first, making long faces, telling of the great hardships they had endured during the winter, pleading for good prices and a little "jawbone." That was the word used throughout the North for credit. Nobody seemed sure of its origin, but some believed it was a hangover from the days of the early French trappers, who in asking for credit might have vouched that they were worthy of it by saying "Je suis bon!" I am good.

When the Indians had unloaded their poorest skins and bought the bare necessities of food and clean clothes, the finer pelts came out, the silky dark mink, the soft voluptuous marten, the otter and fisher and silver fox. With these they bought fancy things—bright head scarves for their women, beads and needles, blouses, sometimes even a gay cotton dress. For themselves they wanted colorful bandannas, a fancy belt or buckle, or overalls. Now and then one would indulge himself in a ten-gallon hat, although for the most part they went bareheaded.

At night they sat around their campfires, watching the meat simmer in the kettles, often singing in the peculiar,

A hunting party returns to Telegraph Creek, 1923. *From the left:* Callbreath's store, the Hyland warehouse, Hyland's store, the Gold Commissioner's office, the Stikine Hotel.

repetitious half-key melody that I would later hear when the packtrain boys were singing on the trail. Finally the leader of the circle would spear a sizable chunk of meat with his knife, grasp it in one hand and bite into a corner of it. Holding it so, he cut a piece off with a swift slashing stroke of the knife, barely missing his own nose. The chunk was then passed to the next man in the circle, who repeated the process, and that continued, the meat going round and round, until all had eaten their fill.

One weekend I walked by myself a dozen miles up the Stikine to the mouth of the Tahltan River. This was the site of the old Indian village of Tahltan, a natural fortress elevated above the surrounding country at the top of a sheer-walled canyon. In winter only a few Indians lived in the village, mostly old people, but now, in summer, it was filled to overflowing with young and old. A wide trail angled down the lava wall of the canyon, emerging at the foot onto a little flat valley where the Tahltan flowed into the Stikine. Here the Indians had their fishing camp. A few log houses sheltered the fishermen, and close by stood huge smokehouses, built of poles set close together in the ground, the walls standing twenty feet high.

Salmon crowded up the Tahltan in almost solid ranks. A few of the older Indians still used handwoven gill nets, but more fished with strange gaff hooks mounted on the ends of long thin poles. The hook was usually made from an old file, heated, hammered into the proper shape and filed to a sharp point. Sometimes it was even equipped with a barb. The end of the shaft was smoothed, heated red hot, and then burned into the end of the pole to assure a snug fit. Next the hook was hung on a twelve-inch length of rawhide fastened to the pole. The whole arrangement amounted to a combination of gaff hook and harpoon. When a salmon was hooked, the hook pulled out of its socket, and no matter how hard the fish fought or how heavy he was, there was no solid resistance to enable him to shake free.

The fish were split lengthwise and hung over pole racks in the smokehouses to smoke over slow fires of green alder and willow. The Indians counted their wealth by the number of fish they smoked. Some had as many as two thousand by fall. This, I was told, was about the time when the old custom of burying fresh fish in pits came to an end. Fish so buried got rotten before they froze in October or November, and dug up in spring, were considered a great luxury. The Tahltans shared this practice with some of the Eskimos of the eastern Arctic, who buried seal meat or seabirds and allowed them to get very high before freezing. Curiously, even white men who spent a few years in the high Arctic came to acquire a taste for such meat and rated it more flavorful than freshly killed game or fish.

I went back to the village a number of times and some of the older Indians and I became good friends. It was from one of them, Casca John, ancient and wrinkled, that I heard a strange story that had long since become a legend in the tribe. The Tahltans had no written language, but it had been handed down from generation to generation for more than a hundred years.

Many years before, Casca John told me, the hated Tlingits from the coast had come up the Stikine, taken the village of Tahltan by surprise and raided it. A great battle had been fought, but in the end many of the young men lay

The Great Glacier on the Stikine, the site of Casca John's story.

dead and many of the young women had been carried away.

Some of the survivors followed the victors downriver after the battle, until they reached the great ice barrier that lay athwart the valley a hundred fifty miles below the village. This had always been considered the natural boundary of Tahltan territory, and in truth the Indians feared the mystery of the river that disappeared into a hole in the ice wall at that point. But now they summoned up courage to clamber over the glacier and reach the outlet on the downstream side. They found that the ice covered the valley for nearly four miles, with the Stikine flowing through a tunnel underneath. On the side of its origin, the glacier came down from ice fields high up among the peaks. On the opposite side of the valley, it extended far enough up the mountain that there was no ready way around it. This enormous barrier of ice, four miles across and hanging two hundred feet above the

river, seamed with crevices and strewn with rocks, formed a natural defense wall against the invaders should they return; the Tahltans were sure they would.

At this point in his story old Casca John rubbed the back of a wrinkled hand across his watery eyes, as if to clear his memory and see back through the misty veil of time. We were sitting on the bank of the river watching his salmon net that evening. From time to time his whole body stiffened and the short stick he held in his hands was bent across his knees, as he lost himself in the tale he was relating.

Each winter after that disastrous raid, he went on, some two hundred Tahltan braves trained for war, rolling and wrestling in the snow, naked except for loincloths, while their elders lashed their backs with rawhide whips to harden them to pain. They danced and ran, chasing one another over broken lava to toughen legs and feet. The longer they could endure this savage training, the more fit they were to defend the village against the hated Tlingits.

Each spring when the ice broke up in the Stikine the defense band went downriver to the ice wall and made ready for battle. The coast Indians would not come sooner than that, for when they raided it would be in their big war canoes. The Tahltans camped among the trees above the glacier, built fires only when the wind was blowing upriver, and then kept the fires low. They carried big boulders and piled them at the lip of the ice cliff overhanging the river, where they could be dropped on any canoe that tried to come through. Scouts were posted on both banks downstream to guard against surprise.

At last, at the dark of the moon in May, the Tlingits came.

Their long war canoes knifed through the boiling current silently and swiftly. Twelve warriors paddled each canoe, swaying in perfect unison, while others rested, waiting their turn. Their faces were daubed with yellow ocher and they wore eagle plumes stained with the ocher and a dull red dye they obtained from cedar roots. At the high prow of each canoe stood a totem of fish or frog or raven, proud and defiant.

The Tahltan scouts counted twenty canoes. Runners went back and the main camp erupted. Five chosen leaders took the two hundred warriors to their stations. A handful of the best bowmen were placed upstream from the ice bridge, to pick off with obsidian-tipped arrows any of the enemy that might make it through the tunnel. Fifty men were sent to cover the banks of the river downstream as well, in the event some of the canoes turned and ran for safety. The rest of the force sprinted across the glacier to their piles of rocks.

Since the tunnel was between three and four miles long, the leaders calculated that all twenty of the enemy canoes, or more if they came, would be under the ice before the first pushed into the open on the upstream side. That provided a natural trap. There was at least a dozen feet of clearance between water and ice roof, but the current was

Hudson Bay John (*left*) and Casca John (*right*), who told me the story of the Great Glacier Battle.

swift in the tunnel and the Tlingit flotilla would move slowly, even though the paddlers redoubled their efforts out of dread of the mystery and echoing darkness of that strange and fearsome place.

When the first Tlingit canoes showed their high prows on the upstream side of the ice wall, three of them appeared almost simultaneously. From the top of the overhang, two hundred feet above them, the wild, shrill war cry of the Tahltans rang out and a storm of rocks went tumbling over the cliff. Some only raised splashes in the water, but some found their mark and went through the thin shells of the cedar dugouts as if the boats had been paper. The three canoes were smashed and overturned in a turmoil of falling boulders, rushing water and brightly painted flung bodies. Arrows and more rocks rained down. Carried swiftly downstream beneath the ice, not a Tlingit from those three canoes escaped death.

Apparently the following canoes believed that the ice wall itself had fallen. They hurried forward, probably wanting only to be out of the tunnel, and they were smashed and destroyed one by one as they emerged. At last a few turned and raced downstream, but showers of rocks and streams of arrows awaited them there as well.

Not a single Tlingit escaped, Casca John declared.

The Tahltans patrolled the river below the ice wall for

days, collecting scalps and searching for Tlingit footprints. Of the latter they found none. That was the last of the great battles between the two tribes. The Tahltans believed they had slain hundreds of their enemy, and the Tlingits had no stomach for raiding upriver again.

Casca John finished his recital. His fists clenched and the stick in his hands snapped. A tremor ran through his body, as if he were throwing off a spell, and he looked away from me to watch his fishnet in the river at our feet.

I might have doubted the whole story, might have set it down as an old man's fanciful account of something that had happened before he was born, but for what happened the next morning. I saw him at his net again, and he beckoned me to him and handed me a crumpled piece of old newspaper.

I opened it carefully, and as the significance of what I held in my hand dawned on me, I gasped in astonishment. It was a very old but brilliantly dyed eagle feather, stained with yellow ocher and dull red, the red that comes only from the roots of the cedar tree—and cedar does not grow on the Stikine above the Great Glacier.

This was a Tlingit feather, an incredibly ancient relic of that long-ago battle at the ice tunnel, handed down to Casca John as the story itself had been, from one generation to the next. I realized that in telling the story to me, a white man, the old Tahltan had done me great honor.

I handed him back the eagle feather and walked wordlessly away, leaving him to his dimly remembered dreams of the past.

4
INTO THE INTERIOR

Beyond the shark-tooth ranges sawing savage at the sky
There's a lowering land no white man ever struck.
—*"The Prospector"*

Even before I reached Telegraph Creek I had a tempting chance to chuck my clerk's job and go prospecting for gold.

Charlie Span, a bearded old-timer with flowing white hair, came aboard the *Hazel B* at the mouth of one of the many creeks we passed. I was told that he was a sniper, a loner who worked the creeks wherever his fancy took him, without staking out a claim of his own. His equipment was a rocker, a small boxlike contraption that he could carry with him. He washed gravel with it by rocking it back and forth, collecting the gold on a piece of canvas or behind cleats nailed across the bottom. The old man took a fancy to me and offered to take me with him for the summer and teach me his trade. But I refused. I had hired out to the Hudson's Bay Company, and I felt bound by my agreement. On top of that, working for the company was for me the fulfillment of a cherished dream.

But two men, Captain Barrington and the owner of the curio shop back at Wrangell, had hinted strongly that I'd soon leave my job for the gold creeks or the trapline. And before the summer ended I was ready to throw in the sponge

Charlie Span, a typical gold sniper, with his rocker and his companion.

and do as they had predicted. I had had the misfortune to fall into the hands of a post factor who could not or would not teach me or any other subordinate anything about the fur trade. And that had been my real reason for taking the job in the first place.

John Boyd, in addition to being chief trader at Telegraph Creek, was in charge of three posts in the interior: Porters Landing at the north end of Dease Lake, McDame Creek down the Dease River, and Lower Post at the junction of the Dease and Liard. I had been hired as a bookkeeper but Boyd would not allow me anywhere near the books. For three months I worked as a flunky, at one servile job after another, cleaning out a dirty warehouse, scrubbing floors, scraping mold off spoiled bacon. I was being paid $125 a month and given a house to live in. That was a good wage for a twenty-two-year-old at that time, but apart from it I was no better off than my friend Jimmy Lowe and another young apprentice. Both had contracted to serve a five-year apprenticeship for their room and board and $5 a

month. Despite the difference in wages, all three of us were
doing the same kind of work and it soon became plain to me
that Boyd did not want a bookkeeper and would not tolerate
a helper of any kind who might interfere with his somewhat
peculiar way of trading.

When he continued to stand me off and I saw that I
would have no chance under him to learn the fur trade, I
went over his head. I wrote to his superior in Vancouver and
asked that I be given the work for which I had been hired.
Nothing came of that, however, so I gave thirty days' notice
of my intention to quit.

Then my big chance came.

A mining engineer by the name of Arthur Brindle, who
had been at the post several times and whom I had gotten
to know quite well, offered me a job as his assistant for the
balance of the season, at better wages than I had been
getting. Even more important, he wanted me to go with him
on a long backpack trip into the interior. He worked for a
Vancouver mining company, and we would be looking at
mining properties. We would go first to Dease Lake, he said,
at the end of the packhorse trail seventy-five miles over the
mountains, and then follow the lake down its entire length
to explore mineral formations along the shore.

Nothing could have delighted me more than the prospect of those weeks of late summer and autumn in the
wilderness, two men on their own. I'd come out far wiser
in the ways of survival, of hunting for food, living on the
trail with the bare minimum of equipment, making little
overnight camps, cooking over an open fire—the things I
had come North in the hope of doing. I'd even learn
something about prospecting and recognizing mineral formations when I saw them, and maybe that would prove even
more valuable than learning the fur trade. On top of all this,
I thoroughly liked Brindle. Slightly built and shorter than I,
he was wiry, glowing with health and tough as rawhide. He
was about forty-five and had been out from England many
years, but still spoke with a North-of-England accent that I
enjoyed. He would be a good trail companion.

The two of us hiked away from Telegraph Creek in late

Prospectors starting out into the Yukon from Telegraph Creek in 1923. The man standing sideways with the pack on his back is Arthur Brindle; at extreme right, on the porch, is John Boyd, my superior at H.B.C.

August, a week after he hired me, carrying sixty-pound packs and following the packhorse trail to Dease Lake. The first few miles were uphill, the August sun was still hot, and sweat poured out of us in streams. Then, just below a narrow raging canyon on the Stikine, we entered the cool shade of spruce forests, the trail dropped away before us, and despite the weight of our packs the hike turned comfortable.

We crossed an ancient shaky bridge over the Tahltan River, just above where it ran into the Stikine. The old people of the Tahltan Indians were fishing there for salmon, and hundreds of fish were drying in their strong-smelling smokehouses.

The second night out I had an encounter of a kind that had to be expected in that country but that was entirely new to me. The effect was startling.

While Arthur got the campfire going, I went to the creek for water and discovered a lush patch of wild raspberries. I returned to get a pailful for our supper and was blissfully picking berries when the head of a big bear rose above the bushes not three feet from me. I could have all but reached out and touched him. We stared each other in the eye for a stunned three or four seconds. Actually I had little to fear, for as luck would have it the bear was a black and not a grizzly. At that distance a grizzly would almost certainly have been on me in a flash. The black was probably as scared as I was. I dropped my pail, he went out of sight in the bushes, and then he was running full tilt one way and I was matching his speed in the opposite direction. When I got back to the campfire, Arthur was doubled over with laughter.

"I didn't know you could move that fast," he told me. On the trail the next day, every now and then he'd break into a loud chuckle—and I knew what he was thinking about.

We traveled steadily, cooling our swollen feet in ice-cold creeks when we stopped for lunch, shooting a grouse or rabbit for supper, rolling into our sleeping bags before dark, bone-tired, up at five and on the trail again by six. I carried a fishline around my hat, and sometimes we varied our evening meal with trout or grayling. Every stream had them, and the country teemed with grouse, rabbits, ducks, moose and bear. It was a rich land, the kind I had dreamed about, wild and unspoiled.

As shadows deepened at dusk, several times I mistook a stump for a black bear, much to Arthur's amusement. But I finally had the last laugh, when one such stump got up off its rump and strolled into the bush. Once we saw a big grizzly, but he was well off the trail, eating berries on an open hillside. Arthur had great respect for his kind, and we went on without letting him know we were there.

We reached the upper end of Dease Lake in less than a week, coming down to the shore at a point opposite a small Indian settlement of half a dozen cabins and a few tents. We were now at the jumping-off place for the interior of the Yukon country. From here a man could go down the Dease

River to the Liard, down the Liard to its junction with the mighty McKenzie at Fort Simpson, and down north on the McKenzie all the way to the Arctic Ocean.

An oldtime Indian known as Packer Tom was camped at Dease Lake with his wife and a big family of children. He had lived at the head of the lake for years and knew the district well. More important to us, he had a rowboat for rent. He called on us, bringing a present of fresh whitefish, and we made a deal for the boat for two or three weeks, for out trip to the foot of the lake.

That afternoon, to the great amusement of the local Indians, I went for a swim, something they would not have dreamed of doing. Instead, they took an occasional sauna-type sweat bath, building a low tent frame shaped like an inverted bowl, covering it with canvas or moose hide, putting heated rocks inside and dashing cold water over the rocks to make dense clouds of steam. The thing that never failed to puzzle me about this custom was the fact that after ten minutes or so in the steam room the Indian would dress in the same sweaty, greasy clothing, often infested with lice,

A packhorse train arrives at Dease Lake (75 miles from Telegraph Creek), the jumping-off point for miners heading into the Yukon Territory.

The pack dogs Arthur Brindle and I used on our trip up Thibert Creek.

that he had worn before, and he promptly smelled as strong as before his once-a-year cleanup.

Our trip down Dease Lake to Porters Landing was uneventful; it consisted mostly of twenty-eight miles of hard rowing. The Landing was a fascinating place, dominated by the Hudson's Bay Company post, with a cluster of scattered cabins belonging to local trappers or prospectors. Most of the cabins had fine gardens, with potatoes, carrots, turnips, and cabbages growing lush and green in the long days of the brief summer. We were warmly entertained for a couple of days, and then we rented four big pack dogs to carry our gear on a trip up Thibert Creek to prospect and look at mining properties.

The dogs were sled animals, weighing one hundred and ten pounds or more, big and strong and hard as nails. And they seemed genuinely pleased at getting away from their kennels and chains, even under pack. I had never seen dogs packed before, and it proved to be an interesting procedure. The packsaddle was much like that used on horses, but of course on a smaller scale. It consisted of a piece of canvas, carefully fitted to the individual dog, with a big pocket, or pannier, on each side. Those panniers contained the load, divided so the weight was equal on each side, and adjusted so that the panniers did not hang too low or rub the dog's legs. A second canvas went over the top, and the whole was lashed in place with two cinches, one that passed under the dog just back of its front legs, the other behind the curve of the belly ahead of the hind legs. The corners of the panniers were held in place by these lashings, after the fashion of the diamond hitch used on packhorses.

The foremost rule was not to overload the dog. Big pack dogs, such as the ones we were renting, could comfortably carry thirty-five or forty pounds day after day, but if overloaded they soon became swaybacked and worthless either for packing or winter sled-pulling. Properly fitted, the packs appeared to be immovable. But I was to learn quickly how a wise old sled dog can rub his pack against a tree and loosen the bindings, and also how thoroughly he can get snagged in brush if he gives unexpected chase to a rabbit.

But despite the minor drawbacks, I can remember few days in my life that I have enjoyed more than that trip.

The country was wild and beautiful, laced with creeks and hung with waterfalls. It was also gold country, and we found many abandoned workings. At one place we even found four men engaged in the hard job of building a long flume from whipsawed lumber. They had worked two years to drain the stream and uncover the bedrock, but we learned later that when they started to dig they found a buried Chinese waterwheel six feet below the surface gravel, covered in times of spring flood. Chinese miners in the very early days had worked out to the last ounce the ground this quartet had sweated and grubbed for two years to get into.

In another place we came on a sniper, a lone miner down on his hands and knees, scraping dirt out of a rock crevice and scooping it into a gold pan with a tablespoon. He was working ground abandoned by a hydraulic mining operation, and he told us he was washing out enough dust and small nuggets to give him a winter's grubstake for his trapline.

Crossing a shaky hand-built bridge across a small tributary of Thibert Creek later that day, we lost one of our pack dogs. He lost his footing, plunged into the fast water and was swept swiftly downstream. We threw off our own packs and raced after him, but thick brush held us back and we did not see him again. Half a mile downstream, however, his wet tracks led out of the water and up the bank. Despite the handicap of his thirty-pound pack, he had survived the tumbling current. Brindle surmised he would head straight for home at Porters Landing, and when we got back there weeks later, we learned that that was exactly what had happened. He had shown up unharmed the same day we lost him, with his pack still on his back. For us, the mishap meant living mainly off the land the rest of the trip, for the lost dog had carried most of our food supplies. But game and fish were plentiful enough that we felt little concern on that score.

At the mouth of Mosquito Creek we reached the cabin of George Adzit, a friend of Arthur's. We had encountered him and his Indian wife while we were rowing down Dease Lake and he had told us that when we got to his cabin we would find plenty of grub and we'd be welcome to help ourselves.

We started to look for the grub but all we could find, either in the cabin or in the high cache outside, was a sack or two of hardened salt and a five-pound box of tea. The cache held nothing but old dog harnesses, steel traps, and ragged blankets. I finally solved the riddle. Going to the creek for water, I found two hindquarters of moose submerged in the running water. The hide had been removed and some of the meat cut away. So this was the plenty of grub the owner of the place had talked about. The meat was so spoiled that I doubted even our dogs would eat it. They did, however, and they were welcome to it.

Dusk had not yet fallen, so I took my rifle, walked a couple of miles up the creek to a small lake, and killed two ducks for our supper. We finished eating and crawled into our sleeping bags. A drizzle of cold rain had set in and the shelter of the cabin was welcome, grub or no grub.

The next morning we went back to the lake where I had killed the ducks, made camp, and settled down to do some serious prospecting.

A "belt" of serpentine rock crossed the country for many miles in this area. To the prospector serpentine is a favorable rock formation to follow, as it is usually associated with other minerals. We climbed the steep grassy slope from our lakeside camp until we plodded over the summit. As we cleared the top a broken wall of rock scarred the mountainside beside us, sloping to a huge valley miles below. The going got rougher as we followed closely against the creviced wall, stumbling over broken rock and boulders, searching the walls for minerals. The smooth green serpentine rock appeared again, its slick shiny surface feeling oily to the touch. Here and there we broke off chunks with the prospector's pick. The serpentine gave way to a sheer wall of schist rock about twenty feet high that followed down the hill toward two tiny lakes shining in the sun like sparkling jewels. Covering the schist wall was a solid mass of white arsenic that made it appear like a milky waterfall. Arthur examined it carefully and a little farther along we found outcroppings of chrome ore. We took pictures of it and many samples, which we loaded in my packsack.

At the edge of the first of the twin lakes we slipped out of our packs and made tea and ate cold grouse left over from the previous night's supper. It was late sundown when we slid down the grassy hillside to our camp.

The next day proved a lucky one for us. We had hardly found our way back to the contact of serpentine and schist rock when we noticed a change in the serpentine. On close examination we found it to contain veinlets of crysotile or asbestos. I peeled the fibers from the bright green rock with my fingernail as we tested the find for a hundred yards or more down the slope. This could be an important discovery although transportation was years away, apparently, from this isolated corner of the wilderness.

So the days went by as we gloried in the beauty and quiet of this clean free land. One day we came to the edge of a lake and watched an old hen mallard leading her flock of chicks away from us, the string of babies following in tandem, making a single wake across the surface of the water. Suddenly the lake erupted not twenty yards from

Arthur standing on the spring-pole bridge over Thibert Creek, where we lost one of our dogs.

where we stood. A huge cow moose head broke the surface with a great splash, her absurdly large ears flopping down from the enormous head, like some cartoon army mule. The dripping head and shoulders cleared the water to show long strands of a dark green weed hanging from either side of her mouth, like whiskers from an old Chinaman. Arthur and I exploded with laughter at the sight, but the moose seemed not to be disturbed by our noise and after chewing the weed awhile she ducked down again, completely submerging below the surface to gather more of the succulent weed.

So this, I thought, is how prospectors live: roaming the hills as freely as the wind, following a contact of favorable geological formations, up hill and down dale, chipping off rock samples from mineral outcroppings and sometimes sampling gravels in creek bottoms for gold; hunting your grub with a rifle and fishing the creeks at night camp; pitching your little mosquito tent beside whatever creek or lake you came to near sundown, while glorying in the super-abundance of health and hardened muscles obtained without trying.

Arthur was generous in sharing his knowledge with me.

Each evening we discussed the samples collected and the formations we had seen. Food was no problem—the country abounded in game. Ptarmigan and grouse were everywhere, the grouse so tame that I killed all we wanted with the .22 rifle we carried. One evening, looking for rabbits for dog food, I came across a family of eight grouse perched in a spruce tree, staring witlessly down at me. I decided to try something I had heard trappers talk about. The grouse were on different limbs, one above another. I shot the lowest one. The rest thrust their necks out as if ready to take off, but did not fly. I picked the next one above and dropped it, and I continued to do that until I had killed six. The last and highest two, probably the parents, finally flew off.

The ptarmigan were not a great deal harder to hunt. It was easy to pick off enough for a meal as they perched on rocks or low brush. Moose and caribou were plentiful, and we finally solved our food problem completely by killing a young bull caribou that we lured within easy range by hiding in tall grass and waving a white cloth over our heads. His curiosity brought him right up to us.

There was at least one grizzly in the neighborhood, too, but he stayed on the opposite side of our little valley, fattening on blueberries, and we did not molest him.

The days slipped away, the chill of autumn came into the air, and we awoke one morning to find an inch of snow on the ground. It was time to leave.

We packed our three dogs, mostly with rock samples now instead of food, and started down our back trail for Porters Landing. There we caught a good breeze and sailed our rowboat to the head of Dease Lake in one morning. Luck was with us again, and at the head of the lake we happened to connect with a hunting packtrain returning to Telegraph Creek. We loaded our outfit on the horses and rode back to town in style, arriving late the fourth day.

For me, the whole trip had been a wonderful experience. And there was still one more interesting interlude to come before freeze-up.

In Arthur's mail he found instructions to examine

another mine forty miles down the Stikine. The weekly river-boat came in, unloaded her cargo, and we boarded her for the run downriver. Compared with the snail's pace of the journey I had made up to Telegraph Creek in May, the downstream speed was astonishing. We left in the early morning and were barely through breakfast when the *Hazel B* swung around in the current and nosed to the bank so we could jump off. The crew tossed us our packsacks, the boat backed off and streaked out of sight around a bend, helped by the tumbling river.

We had come to the cozy log cabin of Groundhog Jackson and his wife. Years before Jackson had discovered, staked out, and sold the coal deposit that came to be known as the Groundhog Coal Fields in British Columbia. Hence his nickname. Now he had some claims up the mountain behind his cabin that were showing promise of gold, and it was Brindle's assignment to take a look.

We stayed a week with Groundhog—four days of it camped in the mountains taking ore samples, the rest of the time enjoying the clean cabin, the excellent meals with fresh vegetables from the garden, and the old man's stories. Wet snow was falling in the high country before we left.

The riverboat picked us up and took us back to Telegraph Creek on her next weekly trip. It was the last run of the year for the *Hazel B,* and we found the town in an uproar. Hunting parties had come in from the mountains, loaded with trophies. The traders and outfitters were making the trophies ready for shipment, the Indians were decked out in their finest, and an air of final celebration before the long isolation of winter hung over the place. Some of the whites would be going outside, some would stay and wait for spring in Telegraph Creek.

A big dance was arranged that night in one of the Indian houses capable of accommodating the crowd. It was a real frontier hoedown, with a young Indian fiddler playing lively old-time tunes, somebody calling square dances, and bearded hunters—some of them millionaires—and bearded miners dancing with the Indian women until they were ready

Looking south over Telegraph Creek at the onset of winter, 1923.

to drop. Not everybody was sober. Some of the women were young and prettty, some were old and wrinkled. It didn't seem to matter.

There was little left of the night when the party broke up. At the first light of morning, the whistle of the *Hazel B* sounded long and loud on the frosty air, and all who were going outside hurried aboard. If they missed this sailing they'd winter where they were whether they wanted to or not.

I had waited until almost the last minute to make up my mind, but I knew now what I wanted to do. I'd stay in Telegraph Creek and see what the winter brought.

I did not regret my decision, but there was something very final about watching that last boat pull out from shore,

swing with the current and head downstream.

I had a fair idea of what lay ahead. In another month the temperature would drop to forty below. If I needed meat I'd hunt my own. If I couldn't find a cabin to live in (I was lucky on that score) I'd have to build one. Whatever happened, there would be no contact with the world outside until the *Hazel B* came back in May.

I stood at the edge of the road looking down on the river, with the other winter residents around me. Men waved from the deck of the boat and we waved back. Just before they went out of sight around the first bend, the captain sent a final lonesome blast of the whistle echoing back from the hills. I suspect it echoed in the hearts of most of those who were left behind, too. I know it echoed in mine.

5

THE FIRST WINTER

Far away, so faint and far, is flaming London, fevered
Paris,
That I fancy I have gained another star.
Far away the din and hurry, far away the sin and
worry,
Far away—God knows they cannot be too far.
—"The Rhyme of the Remittance Man"

With the departure of the last riverboat of the season, the whole atmosphere of Telegraph Creek changed. The little town turned quiet and settled down to its winter isolation.

Left behind were some two hundred Indians, most of whom would leave for their traplines as soon as the snow was deep enough for dogsled travel, and about twenty whites, including the three traders and the telegraph operator and their wives.

The packhorses were driven out to winter pasture, where the snowfall would be light and they could get through until spring on wild hay. The trappers got ready for their traplines and everybody else began stacking up rows and rows of firewood.

I made a deal with a wood hauler to buy wood from me. A road of sorts led out from town four miles to a stand of timber where wood could be cut for the asking. I found that, using a six-foot crosscut saw and an ax, I could cut, trim, and pile a cord a day. It kept me going from daylight until the early darkness settled down, and I'd then walk the four miles back to town or catch a ride on the wood truck.

I needed a meat supply, and one evening I ran into an Indian named Dennis, the head guide for Bob Hyland's hunting business. He was going moose hunting the next day, he said, and if I'd furnish the grub for the two of us I was welcome to go along. He'd show me how it was done. I couldn't have found a better teacher. Dennis had a string of horses. We took a tent, our own supplies, and plenty of horse feed, and rode out to Level Mountain, reaching it the second afternoon. I had done no moose hunting and some of Dennis's methods seemed strange, such as making a big half circle to come up into the wind at a certain place, or walking away from a fresh track in the opposite direction from the way the moose was traveling. But I learned quickly that the Indian knew what he was doing.

I was alone in camp the third day when I heard a sudden loud crashing in brush close by. I grabbed my rifle, sneaked quietly toward the noise, and saw the antlers of a big bull swaying above the willows. Only his head and neck were showing, so I let go at what I could see.

The shot was mostly luck, for I was shaking with excitement and the gun barrel must have been making circles when I squeezed the trigger. The bull fell as if clubbed.

Standing over him, I found myself marveling that such an awkward-looking animal could carry a set of antlers five or six feet wide through the thickest timber at a swinging trot, avoid the trees, and never slacken pace.

Dennis and I killed four moose in the five days we camped there. We built a high cache and left two of them there, quartered and covered with the hides. The two fattest we loaded onto the packhorses, then we headed for home.

We went by way of the Indian village of Tahltan, where Dennis's old parents lived, planning to stay overnight there and leave some meat for the old folks. We were a mile from the village when a salamander scurried across the trail just ahead of our horses. It was a small lizardlike animal and I realized that its appearance at that season of year was un-

Gardner Webb College Library

usual. Dennis reined his horse to a frantic stop and sat staring at the soft bed of pine needles where the salamander had scampered across. The deepest concern showed on his face, and he stabbed a forefinger and said flatly, "Somebody die." He explained in jerky sentences that a salamander crossing your trail is an unfailing sign of death in your family. His wife was expecting a baby any time, and it was she he feared for.

He looked at his watch. "Four o'clock," he said. "I ride to town fast. You stop at Tahltan and leave meat for old folks. The boys there help you pack tomorrow morning, and you come to town." He spurred his horse and was gone, with a thirteen-mile ride ahead.

I spent the night in Tahltan, reloaded the packhorses in the morning and rode to Telegraph Creek. When I entered the Indian settlement we called Drytown, I could see that something was indeed wrong. The Indians who took the horses were silent. One of them motioned me toward Dennis's house.

He met me at the door. "My wife okay," he said. "Got baby. My sister die yesterday afternoon."

To this day, I have no more of an explanation of that strange episode than you have.

For the next two months I kept busy cutting wood and getting used to my first pair of snowshoes, which a local Indian had made for me. I bought a grown Husky bitch with three pups and started to break the pups to harness. I soon had them hauling an empty sled four miles out to the wood-lot.

A week before Christmas I was offered a job that appealed to me.

The Yukon Telegraph Line was then a single wire that stretched from Hazelton, a town on the railroad in central British Columbia, through hundreds of miles of roadless wilderness over the mountains to Telegraph Creek, then north through Atlin, and on to Whitehorse. From there it went down the valley of the Yukon to Dawson City. That wire was the only means of communication Telegraph Creek had with the outside world during the winter months, except for a once-a-month dogsled mail service at Atlin.

Telegraph stations were operated along the line, eighty to a hundred miles apart. An operator and lineman wintered at each station. Between were refuge cabins ten or twelve miles apart, a day's travel for a man on snowshoes.

Once a year packtrains supplied the main stations. The refuge cabins had only wood and kindling, a bunk, table, and stove. If a tree fell across the line, the linemen went out from each side of the break and repaired it, often meeting and working together. But in rough weather it was likely to be down as long as three weeks at a time.

In mid-December the operator at Telegraph Creek came to me and offered me the job of backpacking fifty pounds of mail to Raspberry Creek, a station forty miles south. The lineman from Iskoot station, still farther south, would meet me there. I'd use the refuge cabins for my overnight stops.

I hiked away from Telegraph Creek on a crisp winter morning, with the mail, an eiderdown sleeping bag, half a slab of bacon, a little flour, salt, and tea in my pack. I was carrying a .22 and counted on supplementing my meager rations with grouse or rabbits. It did not enter my mind that before the trip was over I would be as close to death as I had ever come.

Two miles out of town, I stopped for a cup of tea with an Indian trapper and his wife. Up to that point I had followed a well-broken trail. When I started on, I had to break my own. The snow was deep and soft, the going hard, and it wasn't easy to follow under the telegraph wire that was my only guide. It was getting dark when I saw Sheep Creek cabin, the first refuge stop, pushed the door open and took shelter for the night.

I was on the trail by starlight, before daybreak the next morning. By early afternoon the temperature, which had stood at twenty below during the night, had moderated and by late afternoon the softening snow was sticking to the webbing of my snowshoes and giving me a bad time. I slogged into the next refuge cabin, at Deep Creek, just before dark, completely worn out.

The next morning I left again before daylight and ran into trouble almost at once. Within an hour the wet snow began balling under my snowshoes. I cut a dry stick, and at each step as I lifted the shoe I whacked it and knocked the snow loose. It was slow going and hard work, but I kept on.

Before noon a heavy wet snow began to fall, and now the rawhide of the snowshoes began to stretch, so that they no longer supported my moccasins. My feet were actually dropping through the webbing with every step I took. I tried to repair the lacing, but the knots blistered my feet almost at once. And then the wind came up, driving the snow into my face until I could no longer keep track of the wire overhead. Late that afternoon, in desperation, I tied a length of rawhide to the toe of each shoe and pulled them up out of the wet snow, one after another, as I staggered along.

I should have stopped and made camp in heavy timber, where I was sheltered from the storm. But I had romantic notions about the mail getting through on time, and I was sure that the station at Raspberry Creek was just over the next ridge, so I kept going. At dark, hardly more than half conscious, I realized with stark terror that I had strayed from the telegraph line. I was lost. I came into a big burn where windfalls tripped me time after time. The last time I looked at my watch it said ten o'clock. I had been fifteen hours on the trail, in the worst possible kind of going. I do not know how long it was after that—but I think not long— when I fell unconscious in the snow and did not get up.

To sleep as I did, under such conditions as that, is supposed to be certain death. But in the darkness of early morning, I awoke, dazed, and hardly knowing where I was. I pinched my arm to test it for feeling, felt nothing, and concluded I was dead. Then, pushing up my head, I saw stars above and heard a dead tree fall. I raised up on one elbow and looked around me.

The sky was clear now, but there had been a heavy fall of snow during the night, for I was buried under nearly a foot of it. Almost certainly it was that covering that had saved me from freezing to death, for I learned later that the temperature had dropped between dusk and dawn that night from forty degrees above to thirty-five below.

My packsack was still hanging on my shoulders, badly torn, and dimly I remembered ripping it on a broken limb shortly before I lost consciousness. My sleeping bag and food were gone but my ax still hung between the shoulder straps. I had the .22, clutched in one hand, and a fistful of shells in a pocket.

I had left a rutted track in the snow the night before, and despite the new snow that had fallen I could still follow it. Half a mile back I found my bedroll and dug in the snow with a snowshoe for the missing grub, but there was no trace of it. I backtracked myself for two miles before I came on the telegraph line. Then I turned and followed it south, making better time now because the cold had turned the snow dry. In an hour I topped a high knoll, looked down a long slope, and saw a tent on a framework of heavy poles, standing in the middle of a little flat. Snow was drifted fifteen feet deep on one side and eddies of the stuff had walled up the back end and the other side. But the entrance was clear. I walked down and went in. I had reached the Iskoot Summit refuge camp, fifteen miles beyond my destination at Raspberry Creek. In the darkness and storm I had passed the station there without knowing it.

There were supplies here—not everything I needed but half a sack of flour, plenty of dry wood, and a can of matches. I melted snow for water, made a crude bannock, and baked it on top of the stove. While I was eating I remembered that this was Christmas Day, my first Christmas in the North. Well, I wasn't lying dead back there under a foot of snow, bait for the wolves, and I could hardly ask for a better Christmas present than that.

I fell into the bunk and slept ten hours, made another flour-paste bannock and repaired my snowshoes as best I could. The lineman who was supposed to meet me had not shown up, so I hung the mail sack from the ridgepole of the tent and set out on my back trail for Telegraph Creek.

Fifteen miles along on the trail, I found where I had passed the Raspberry Creek station in the darkness the night before. I had tramped by within a hundred feet of it.

Two days later I was back in Telegraph Creek. The telegraph operator there was getting ready to send men out to look for me.

I moved to a vacant cabin six miles downriver, chinked it with fresh moss, papered the inside with wrapping paper from the Hudson's Bay Company store, and settled down to train my dog team.

The standard dogsled used in that area then was eight feet long, with steel-shod runners and a platform or bed supported on short hardwood posts. Handles at the back end enabled the driver to steer the sled, and a jerk line, a twenty-foot length of half-inch rope, was fastened to the front end and allowed to trail behind, so that a driver on snowshoes could hold onto it and avoid the danger of being left behind if his team suddenly bolted after a moose.

The Yukon hitch was different from the fan hitch used by the Eskimos in the eastern Arctic. In the Yukon and Alaska, the dogs were harnessed single file between a pair of traces, and sometimes a pair of light pole shafts ran out from the sled to the first dog, enabling him to help in turning right or left. In the fan hitch, an individual line ran back from each dog to a loop of heavy leather at the front of the sled, so that the team ran fanned out, each dog pulling by himself.

The teams were driven entirely by voice. The dog that did not learn to go at "Mush!," stop at "Whoa!," turn right at "Gee!," and left at "Haw!" was soon gotten rid of.

In all the years I was in the North, the only times I ever saw a dog whip used were in the movies. The dog mushers I knew, white and Indian alike, did not even carry a whip. There was now and then a harsh exception to the rule: one winter mail carrier at Telegraph Creek killed a dog or two on almost every trip he made. He would fly into an insane rage and beat the poor brutes to death with an ax handle.

My pups came of a good bloodline, and training them was a joy. I soon had them and their mother hauling firewood to the cabin, and when I killed a moose they brought it home in two-hundred-pound loads.

Only once in the four months I lived alone in the cabin did I go to town for supplies. There was no need. In addition to an abundance of moose meat, I killed a goat, and two trappers on a creek a few miles downriver traded me half a sheep. I fished through the ice in the pool where my creek ran into the Stikine and caught trout whenever I wanted them. Food was never a problem.

Toward the end of the winter, when the lengthening days and warm sun began to foretell the coming of spring, I took one of my dogs, Rogue, and went for a long hike back in the foothills to hunt grouse. It was a good afternoon, and when I started home in late afternoon, I had four or five birds in my packsack. About four or five miles from my cabin I came to a small lake. The ice was now a smooth glare and I took off my snowshoes and started across. The low sun was almost level, reflecting off the surface blindingly bright, and before I reached the far end of the lake a mile away my eyes were burning as if someone had thrown sand into them. I walked ashore and sat down to rest; the pain became almost unbearable. In a very few minutes I was totally blind.

I was three miles from the cabin, with no trail. All I could do was go by the downhill slope of the land and the feel of the sun's warmth. But the sun was setting now, and I wouldn't have it to guide me. If I simply headed for the river, I'd cross the trail to town. Would I feel it under my moccasins? Or would the dog turn into it?

That gave me an idea. Maybe Rogue knew the way home. I'd try him. I fastened my belt around his neck, hung onto one end, and with a little encouragement he got the idea and we started off. I blundered into trees and tangled my snowshoes in brush, but as often as I fell the dog waited patiently. It took us an hour to reach the cabin and by that time the sun was long gone, but the oncoming darkness made no difference to me.

Rogue, the dog who saved me from snow blindness.

For the next ten days I was a blinded cripple, alone and unsure of my fate. Luckily I was an orderly person, who had a place for everything and kept everything in its place. I had plenty of wood and kindling cut, and I knew where every pot hung and every package of food stood in the cupboard.

The hardest job was feeding the dogs. I had no dried fish for them, and I had to climb the ten-foot ladder to the cache and throw down a frozen quarter of moose, chop off each dog's portion with the ax, and carry what was left back up the ladder.

Cooking was no easy task, either, but I made out by feel. I lost track of the days, but at the end of about a week and a half I could open my eyes for a second or two at a time, and thereafter they began to improve slowly. It was a full two weeks before they were of much use to me again.

An Indian trapper told me when it was all over that I could have avoided the snow blindness by blackening my eyelids with a piece of charcoal or wearing primitive goggles made of thin pieces of wood, with a very small aperture in each piece to see through.

The cheechako had learned one more important lesson on the road to becoming a sourdough.

6
THE CLAIM THAT FAILED

*Gold! We leapt from our benches. Gold! We sprang
    from our stools.*
*Gold! We wheeled in the furrow, fired with the faith
    of fools.*

—*"The Trail of Ninety-Eight"*

When the first boat came up the Stikine in May of 1924, it brought word from Arthur Brindle that he would not be coming north that year.

I was still turning over in my mind the ways I wanted to spend the summer when a grizzled old prospector (whose name for once I failed to record in my diary and can no longer remember) came to me and offered me good wages for packing a load of supplies seventy-five miles to Dease Lake. He explained that he wanted to get there ahead of two men who had left the day before, in order to stake a promising gold claim that he believed they had their eyes on. Men racing one another for choice claims was a common enough situation in that day.

A packhorse would have been too slow, but the old man thought I and my dogs could make it. He offered to double my wages if we got to the foot of Dease Lake first. I agreed to try, taking a total load of one hundred twenty pounds between the dogs and myself. Each of the young dogs would carry twenty pounds, the bitch thirty, and I would take the remaining thirty. The prospector would carry his gun and bedroll.

We left Telegraph Creek in late afternoon and hiked steadily, stopping every four hours for a pail of tea and a brief rest. At sunup the next morning we were at the half-way mark and I was sure we would win the race. We figured the men ahead would travel twenty-five miles a day and take three days to reach Dease Lake. They would sleep at the head of the lake the third night, and on the fourth day they would travel down the lake and stake the claims they were after. But by that time we would be ahead of them. With half the hike behind us, we could cover the seventy-five miles to the head of the lake in thirty hours, less than two days to their three. We'd arrive in the night while they were asleep, and by morning we'd be well on our way down the lake by boat.

At the halfway mark we gave ourselves and the dogs a full hour of rest, and then swung out again. The dogs lagged at the end but I encouraged them, and just before midnight we filed down the long grassy slope to Dease Lake, well ahead of the tough schedule we had set ourselves. Fortunately for us, the Hudson's Bay Company packtrain was there and the horses were grazing on new grass, their bells clanging, so our arrival caused no stir.

I took the packs off the dogs, tied them to trees back from the lake, left the prospector with them and walked along the beach to find Packer Tom, the owner of the boat Brindle and I had used the previous summer. He was at home, glad to see me again, and the deal was quickly made. We rowed back past the sleeping tent camp, loaded the prospector and his supplies into the boat, and he and Packer Tom disappeared in the darkness. Richer by fifty dollars and very happy, I stripped and went for an exuberant swim before I rolled up in my sleeping bag. I never learned whether the old man's claim paid off well enough to make the race worthwhile.

In 1925 a mining company built this "road" over the old packhorse trail for tractors like the one on page 60.

Before that year was out I had a gold claim of my own.

I worked that summer for a mining company that was punching what was called, with considerable license, a road, through the mountains from Telegraph Creek to Dease Lake, following the packhorse trail uphill and down. There were stretches of that road that were better suited to canoe travel than tractor, and it was as hard a summer as I have ever put in. I remember one incident in particular.

Frank Ferries, the tractor driver I was working with, undertook to pull two heavily loaded wagons up a steep and muddy hill. The tractor had steel wheels in front, intended to hold the road and permit steering. The rear wheels were caterpillar treads, carried over a triangle-shaped set of sprocket wheels and rollers. Before he started up the hill Frank rigged a coil of half-inch steel cable over the radiator in the hope of holding the front end down. It may have helped, but the front wheels only touched the ground every few feet, and the tractor fought its way to the top like a stiff-legged, clanking kangaroo.

The first tractor train to arrive at Dease Lake over the 75-mile road from Telegraph Creek.

On the next hill a heavy drawbar broke, and it fell to me to hike sixty miles back to Telegraph Creek and pack out a replacement.

I made it to town in two days. Only then did I learn that the drawbar weighed eighty pounds. I padded my packboard with my bedroll, tied the bar on top, and literally staggered off with it. It took me three days to make the return trip, and for a week afterward my spine felt as if it had been telescoped.

I made what I intended would be my last trip to Dease Lake in September, with my four dogs, all of us packing heavy loads. I planned to winter on Thibert Creek with a miner whom Arthur Brindle and I had encountered the previous summer.

Fall rains had set in now and the trail was more of a canal than a pack road, rutted and cut up by the wagons and tractors that had passed over it. I was making camp at the Tanzilla River one evening, dog-tired, when I saw two bearded prospectors slipping and sliding down a long hill toward me, reeling under huge packs.

They were Hugh Ford and Bill Grady, two men whom I had seen often in Telegraph Creek, and they had a story to tell.

They had been out all summer, prospecting on the headwaters of the Eagle River twenty miles beyond the head of Dease Lake, and they had made a strike. On a little creek almost small enough to jump across they had seen color in their pan, and when they dug down four feet to bedrock they hit coarse nuggets. They had staked their discovery claims and were on the way to Telegraph Creek now to record them with the Gold Commissioner.

We talked over hot tea, squatted beside my fire, and Grady reached into his packsack and took out their poke of gold. It was a sack of tanned moose hide about eight inches long and three inches thick. He opened it and spilled the nuggets out onto a canvas ground sheet.

In the evening dusk the campfire made them flash and sparkle and when I touched them and weighed the bigger ones in my hand, a shock went through me like an electric current.

It has been fifty years since that autumn evening on the Dease Lake trail, and I still find myself wondering at the lure of gold and the magic it works.

Surely it must have some mystical quality apart from its worth. It kindles a fire in the blood of men who find it, it whispers, "Make me your god and I will give you your heart's desire." The promise is seldom kept, but there are few men who can resist that seductive whisper. They have responded to it since the dawn of civilization, staking their every possession and even life itself in mad races to be first to reach the glittering yellow metal. I know how it is. Holding those nuggets in my hand there beside my lonely fire, I yielded completely to gold fever.

Ford and Grady had stopped the night before at Dease Lake and shown their gold to a handful of prospectors camped there. Those men were already on the way to the new diggings. By now the word had reached Porters Landing and spread down the Dease River. A real gold stampede would be on—as miners from every creek in the area reacted to the magic cry of "Strike!"

I knew what I must do.

The rain let up by morning and I rose at first light. Hurriedly I built a small cache close to the trail and put most of my outfit in it. I would come back for it after my claim was staked. I hiked away from the Tanzilla carrying only an ax, gun, and bedroll, with my dogs under very light pack. Everything depended on reaching that little creek ahead of the miners from down the Dease.

It was twenty-five miles from my camp to the turnoff where a trail to the Eagle River valley left the one I was following. The tracks of boots and moccasins in the soft mud there told me that some of the stampeders were ahead of me.

I halted long enough to make tea and roast a grouse on a forked stick in front of a fire. I shot rabbits for the dogs, took their packs off to give them a rest, and in two hours we hit out again.

There was a moon, but it went behind a cloud and the night turned too dark for travel on the rough trail we were following. Win or lose the frantic race, I had to stop and make camp. I consoled myself with the knowledge that others behind me on the trail would have to do the same thing.

We were away at early daylight and I pushed the dogs and myself to the limit. In late afternoon we came into the valley of the Little Eagle, and six miles farther on we were at the mouth of the creek where Ford and Grady had made their strike. They had found an old rusted goldpan stuck in the forks of a gnarled spruce tree there, and had given the little stream the name of Goldpan Creek. That name was recorded and has stuck to this day.

Turning up the creek, I saw half a dozen campfires, their smoke curling straight up in the crisp, windless evening. The miners were all from around Dease Lake and I knew every one of them. Ten claims had been staked above Discovery, but I had won my race with the Dease River contingent.

At first light I cut stakes, paced off the 250-foot length up and down the creek and the 1,000-foot width for a placer claim, and wrote my name, date, and license number on the corner post. Last of all, I added the name of the claim, Eleven above Discovery. That was one of the happiest minutes of my life. I owned my own gold claim!

I rested my dogs the next two days while I scouted the area for game and firewood. There was plenty of both. I had the winter ahead for packing in supplies. When spring came I could start digging gold. But first, of course, I had to go back to Telegraph Creek and record my claim. By the time I left the creek, claims had been staked to Twenty-two above Discovery.

The dogs and I took our time going back. The last boat of the year was tied at the bank when we arrived in Telegraph Creek and passengers were carrying their duffle aboard, but I hardly looked in their direction. The Outside held no attraction for me now. I would need the long winter to do all that had to be done.

I went first to the office of Harry Dodd, the Gold Commissioner, paid the modest fee and became the legal owner of Eleven above Discovery.

In the years ahead I would have much dealing with Dodd, and I met no man in the North whom I came to respect more.

When I first encountered him, in the spring of 1923, he had been Gold Commissioner of the Cassiar Mining District for more than twenty-five years, his beginnings going back to the Klondike stampede of 1898. It was years before any other authority came to the district, and Dodd stood alone for law and order in what could well have been a lawless land.

The district was vast, but it had a population of fewer than a hundred whites and perhaps a thousand Indians. They brought their troubles to Harry Dodd and he served as friend, father confessor, and adviser. He also served as lawyer and a stern but just and benevolent judge. I do not know on what legal foundation his authority rested, apart

Harry Dodd, Cassiar District Gold Commissioner, for thirty years the only law in a 78,000-square-mile wilderness.

from matters concerning gold claims, but it was never questioned.

I recall one spring when a report came in that an Indian at the mouth of the Dease River, two hundred fifty miles from Telegraph Creek, had stolen furs from another Indian's traps during the winter. With the breakup he had moved another fifty miles down the Liard, below Lower Post. Quietly Dodd sent word for the Indian to come and see him. It would be a three-hundred-mile walk. The message went by word of mouth, by the marvelous moccasin telegraph whose workings often seemed incredible. It was given to an Indian packtrain boss going to Dease Lake. He passed it on to a prospector who chanced to be going down the Dease River as far as McDame Creek. The next leg it was carried via a Hudson's Bay poling barge returning to Lower Post, and the trader there relayed the word the last fifty miles by local Indians. It was five weeks after Dodd sent out the order before it reached the offender in his fishing camp. Two days later he started for Telegraph Creek.

He did not dare to ignore the summons if he wanted to, for he knew that Dodd could have his credit cut off at the posts and end his trading furs for salt, tea, and traps. With no written order and no escort, he walked that three hundred miles through the mountains and across the rivers to face whatever might be in store for him.

Half a dozen of us were talking in front of one of the trading posts when he trudged into town and headed for the commissioner's office. A few minutes later Dodd stepped out on his porch and called to us.

When we were seated around the office, he announced, "This is a trial. Court is open."

He recited the charge, explained it to the Indian through a trapper interpreter, and asked a few questions. Confession came quickly. The Indian admitted that he had traded furs not caught in his own traps, and Dodd handed down the sentence without any fuss.

"Two months at hard labor," he announced.

There was no real jail at Telegraph Creek. The nearest was at Prince Rupert on the British Columbia coast more than three hundred miles away. There was no thought of sending the Indian there.

We had what passed for a jail, a twelve-by-twelve tent with a lumber floor, at the end of Dodd's garden. It had a stove, pole bunk, table, and two chairs. The prisoner was lodged there and supplied with food which he cooked himself. Cordwood was brought in and he was equipped with an ax and crosscut saw. For two months he cut four-foot logs into stovewood length and split and stacked them. He was free to go to the post when he pleased and to get his own water. In fact he was not confined in any way. But there was no thought he would run off. He served out his sentence and was released in time to go back for his winter's trapping.

I knew that when spring came I would need lumber at my claim for a flume and sluice boxes. A sluice box for pick-and-shovel mining needed to be twelve feet long. That called for boards of that length. I could pack them on a dog-sled toward the end of winter, once the snow was packed and travel conditions became good. I acquired two more big dogs that matched my team, and started storing and drying lumber from a local sawmill.

Many things happened at Goldpan Creek that winter. News of the gold strike spread to the Outside and wild rumors sprang up. Old-timers came in by dog team over the snows from Dawson City, Fairbanks, and other towns. One enterprising arrival, not willing to trust to the luck of mining, built a crude roadhouse at the mouth of the creek, putting up a big tent with pole bunks, benches, and table. He built a cache, hauled in meat and firewood, and by mid-April he had the place ready for business.

I still recall the sign he put up the day after the first packtrain arrived: "Eggs, $1 each. Meal with eggs, $2." For one dollar you got a whole egg of uncertain age. Those that had been cracked or broken on the way in went into the meals with eggs. Meals consisted of moose or caribou meat with potato and a canned vegetable, and cost one dollar. A dollar also paid for a bunk overnight, but the traveler had to supply his own bedroll and he got no sheets or frills.

Tents were strung for a mile up the creek now, new-comers were arriving daily, and from the time the first pack-train came in the roadhouse did a thriving business.

As soon as the snow crusted in March I began my own hauling. It was a hundred miles from Telegraph Creek to my claim, and I made five round trips, the last one just be-fore the south slopes turned bare under the spring sun. At the claim I found a snow-filled crevice in a rock wall where meat would keep through most of the summer. I killed a moose and caribou and stashed the quarters there. Then, to avoid the problem of dog food, I drove my team back to Telegraph Creek and left them with Setsuzo Matsurra, the owner of the old Stikine Hotel, later burned and never re-built, to be fed until I came out in the fall. I hiked back on a thawing trail and got ready to mine.

Through the short Arctic summer I dug and grubbed, built a dam, cut trenches down to bedrock, washed gravel,

Panning my first gold at Eleven above Discovery on Goldpan Creek. I sold the claim for a plug of tobacco and a pound of tea.

and looked for gold. The creek worked for me twenty-four hours a day cutting the gravels down where I had started, and my own working time was only a few hours shorter. Every pan I tested showed traces of dust, but never enough to qualify as pay dirt. For a mile up the creek other men were working just as hard, but with a few lucky exceptions they were doing no better than I. Only once or twice that whole summer did I find a nugget big enough to ring when dropped into the pan.

It was almost autumn when a stranger, a tall Scot, walked in one evening while I was cooking a caribou steak for supper. He asked to camp on my claim while he looked around. I made him welcome, we shared the steak, and he stayed on for a week, helping me dig and test. At the end of that time I had had enough. My total take of gold for the summer was less than two ounces. But the Scot thought the claim still stood a chance and he wanted to buy it.

I had raced other stampeders for that claim, traveled a thousand miles by dog team packing in lumber for it, and sweated and slaved through an entire summer. In the end I sold it to him for a pound of tea and a half-pound plug of pipe tobacco.

In that brief, bitter experience is told much of the story of gold stampedes.

But at Dease Lake, on the way back to Telegraph Creek, I saw the tents of stampeders strung all along the shore. Most of them were cheechakos from Outside, fired with the dream of gold, working at the unaccustomed job of loading pack dogs or lurching off over the muddy trail with backbreaking loads on packboards.

The dream dies hard—as many of them were to prove.

7
THE "COME WHAT MAY"

We built our boats and we launched them. Never has
been such a fleet;
A packing-case for a bottom, a mackinaw for a sheet.
—"The Trail of Ninety-Eight"

I was at Dease Lake in June of 1925 when the second
Hudson's Bay tractor train of the year came in. Who should
be riding on top of the load but Amos Godfrey, the old-
timer with whom I had shared a room at Wrangell two
years before and whom I now counted among my good
friends.

As soon as he saw me he hurried over with exciting
news. He had an Indian with him, Little Jimmy, and he
explained that the Indian had brought him a sample of high-
grade silver-lead ore earlier that spring. Now he had made
a deal with a Vancouver mining company to locate the
deposit precisely and find out more about its extent. It was
somewhere in the Frances Lake area, on the upper waters
of the Liard River, between three hundred and four hundred miles across the mountains. Amos could not make the
trip alone. Would I go with him?

Of course I would. We shook hands on it beside my
little campfire while we ate a supper of fresh whitefish.

It would be a boat trip, into country totally wild and unknown, still a blank space on government maps. So far as we could learn no white men had been there with the exception of the early explorers of the Hudson's Bay Company many years before. All that was known of it was rumor, and the rumors were not exactly reassuring. We heard stories of prospectors who had headed into it and never been heard from, probably drowned in the rapids, and of unfriendly and even dangerous Indians who wanted no white men trespassing in their hunting grounds. Well, we'd go and see.

We'd go down Dease Lake and the Dease River to the Liard, upstream on the Liard to the Frances, and on up that river to Frances Lake.

There were no boats for sale at Dease Lake, and no boatbuilders. We'd have to build our own, whipsawing the green lumber for it. The first thing the next morning we walked the shore until we found a stand of straight-grained spruce that suited us, set up camp there, and went to work.

I have always believed that whipsawing was the invention of the devil, and I still think so.

The first step was to select four heavy, evenly spaced trees that formed a rectangle, for our sawpit. We cut them about six feet above the ground, and on the stumps we notched and set four logs for a frame eight feet long and four wide. Next, on one side we spliced in two long poles that sloped down to the ground. They made skids on which we could roll logs to the top of the frame. That completed the pit.

We chose our trees carefully, picking clear timber without limbs for at least fifteen to eighteen feet above the ground. Our plans called for a poling boat twenty-eight feet in length, blunt at both ends, thirty inches wide on the bottom, with the sides flaring out to about thirty-six inches at the gunwales.

That was all the flare we could afford. The sides of a poling boat had to be nearly vertical, to allow a man to stand erect and put his full weight on a sixteen-foot pole braced against the river bottom. If the sides flared much he'd have to lean out too far.

Pulling the *Come What May* over the rocks around a canyon on the Frances.

All upstream travel would have to be by poling, with one man in the bow and one in the stern. We'd make and carry oars, but they could be used only in rowing downstream or crossing lakes or rivers. A heavy boat of that kind could not be rowed against even a five-mile current, and most of the water we'd be on would be far faster than that.

Finally, the bow of the boat had to be raised in the form of a shovel to allow it to ride over waves when going upstream in fast water.

We rolled the first fifteen-foot log up on the sawpit frame and peeled off the bark with an ax. Next we blackened a length of string with a piece of charcoal, to use as a carpenter uses a chalk line. By stretching the string taut the full length of the log, fastening the ends, lifting the middle a couple of inches and letting it snap back, we got a straight black line for the whipsaw to follow. Next we rolled the log over and repeated the procedure on the opposite side. That gave us two lines that showed where the first slab would be cut off, and by repeating that on all four sides we could

square our log. After that we'd use our charcoal line to mark
off boards of the thickness we wanted.

Amos had brought a seven-foot whipsaw from Telegraph Creek. It was an instrument of torture, with handles
set at right angles to the blade at each end to form a T.
To use it one man had to stand on the sawpit frame, the
other in the pit below. They pulled the saw up and down
like a crosscut, keeping it vertical. It was the responsibility
of the top man to guide the blade along the black line on
his side, while the man in the pit did the same on the under
side of the log. It called for watchfulness and care, but
expert sawmen could cut boards of astonishingly even
thickness.

To say that it was hard and disagreeable work is a
total understatement. Neither man could take his eyes off
that black mark. The upstroke was harder than the down,
and more than once I have seen the man above pull the saw
up through the cut and his breakfast come up at the same
time, from the bending and labor. As for the man in the pit,
though the work wasn't quite so backbreaking for him he
got sawdust in his eyes and down his neck, and the sawdust
was full of pitch. It mixed with his sweat, so that it stuck
and itched wherever it found its way. And for both men
mosquitoes made life an agony they had to endure, since
they could not take their hands off the saw handles to fight
the hungry hordes away.

Every once in a while as Amos and I toiled, the heat
of the spring sun, the sawdust, and the insects became too
much to endure and I called a halt and walked into the lake,
clothes and all. The ice had been out about five weeks and
the worst of the chill was gone, but the water was still cold
enough to refresh and invigorate a man.

We cut our boards of varying lengths, so that the joints
would not all come in one place. We were going into dangerous water and wanted all the strength we could give the
boat.

We cut knees and built a frame, bent some of the green
boards in the curve we would need for the high bow, lashed
them in shape and stood them up to dry in the sun. We

hewed out a big sweep, shaped like an oar but ten feet long, for steering, and set two posts in the stern for it to rest between.

We sweated and slaved through the hot days of early summer, whipsawing, then fastening the boards to the boat's frame with long screws. The high-rising bow took shape and at last the boat was ready for caulking. We collected spruce pitch in discarded jam jars, melted it and mixed it with hot moose fat. I fashioned a crude caulking tool from a piece of dry alder, we unraveled a half-inch rope until the fibers were loose, dipped them into the mixture, and tamped them tightly into the cracks between the boards. They made a perfect waterproof seal.

Amos was about fifty years old at that time, but through all those long hard days he worked as hard as I did, and with fifteen years in the North behind him, he showed far more understanding than I of what lay ahead and of the requirements of our boat and equipment.

While we worked rumors of new gold strikes kept drifting in, and many times we found ourselves tempted to give up our plans and head out for the creeks. The will-o'-the-wisp of gold exerts a strong pull on men. But each time we talked ourselves into staying with the job we had taken on instead.

Fourteen days after we cut the first board our boat went into the water. We named it the *Come What May*, and that was to prove a very appropriate choice.

The last step in our preparations was to make two oars and a spare steering sweep, cut and shape with a drawknife two poles of dry spruce sixteen feet long, shaved thin enough to fit easily in the hands. We rigged a mast through the forward seat, sewed a sheet of canvas to the half-inch line for a sail, and we were ready to start.

I was looking forward to this great adventure. Amos was not given to talking and I still do not know what his thoughts were, but I am sure he had fewer romantic notions than I. I am also sure that his reasons were sound. I'd learn that before the trip was finished.

Daybreak mist still drifted across Dease Lake in ghostly

streamers when we shoved off. At sunrise a breeze came up and we hoisted our sail. We ran the length of the lake, twenty-eight miles, in five hours, passed the post at Porters Landing without stopping, and headed directly into the Dease River. Amos manned the long sweep while I rowed, but the current swept us along and I needed to row only enough to keep steerageway.

The Dease was a beautiful river, with heavy spruce forest coming to the water's edge, high mountains in the background, and small creeks running in every few miles. There were ducks and moose in the sloughs, black bears on the gravel bars, eagles and ravens overhead, and none of them showed much fear of the boat drifting swiftly downstream. I told myself again, as I had so often in the past two years, that this untamed land was what the Garden of Eden must have been.

If the Dease was beautiful, it was also dangerous in places. We made camp the first night where the Cottonwood River came in from the west and Amos, who knew this part of our route well, led the way down the bank a short distance for a look at the Cottonwood Rapids that we'd confront the first thing in the morning. They had a bad name and deserved it. Throughout the years they had taken a fair toll of miners, traders, and trappers passing down the Dease.

When we reached a place on shore where we could look down the reach of tumbling water, I could see that the danger lay in a string of big boulders that stretched diagonally across the river from shore to shore. About halfway across, one huge rock stood up above the foaming current: that would be the worst place of all. A boat driven against that rock would be smashed or swamped, and missing it would call for tricky work at the oars and sweep. But the alternative was to portage boat and outfit around the rapids, and that was too hard a job. Our boat had not been built for carrying.

The next morning, as soon as we had eaten breakfast, we let the current carry us down and we put the high nose of the *Come What May* into the cauldron of white water. I rowed as I had never rowed in my life and Amos worked the sweep with his last ounce of strength. Just above the big rock we almost turned sidewise, something we both knew meant disaster. But we strained at our work, righted the boat, and swept past that great boulder so close we all but scraped it. I could have struck it with my hand as we knifed by. A minute later we were floating in smooth water below the rapids and I rested on the oars and got my breath back.

That was my introduction to white water. At the moment I thought we had had a very close call, and I suppose we had. But before the summer ended I would see canyons and rapids that would make the Cottonwood run seem like a safe ride on a roller coaster.

At the McDame Creek Post of the Hudson's Bay Company we tied up and were greeted by Mike Larsen, the trader in charge. Half a dozen cabins were scattered over a meadow beside the post, Indian children were playing nearby, and there were dogs all over the place, not all of them tied.

It was the shedding season, and I had never seen a worse-looking lot of sled dogs—unfed, half starved, and gaunt. Where patches of fur had been rubbed away I could count their ribs through the tightly drawn skin. Small wonder that Indian dogs were such expert thieves, I reflected. They acquired great cunning at an early age. They had to, to survive. I have seen one snitch a can of evaporated milk, puncture it with his teeth, tilt it up in almost human fashion and drink the contents to the last drop. Even as puppies they learned to pull boxes or chairs into place and stand on them to reach bacon or a ham hanging on a ceiling wire, and many of them even mastered the trick of pulling a latchstring in order to open a cabin door.

There was a vacant cabin at the post belonging to a friend of Amos, and we camped in it for the night.

Amos had not been down the Dease below McDame Creek. From here on, all the way to our destination in the Frances Lake country, the rivers and their rapids would be totally new to both of us. All we knew was that we could expect plenty of bad water.

Before we left the McDame Creek Post, Larsen told us there were two canyons in the last few miles of the Dease, just upstream from the Lower Post at its confluence with the Liard. Both were dangerous, he warned. He said nothing about another spot, just around the first bend below McDame Creek, that would give us a very bad scare.

We left the post in late afternoon, intending to make a few miles downstream before camping. We rounded that first bend, and ahead of us a shallow rapids, too rock-broken for our boat, was foaming more than halfway across the river. The rest of the current knifed through a narrow crevice between walls of rock, a short, sheer canyon. It had enough room for the boat, and although the current ran like a millrace, the water was smooth.

We headed into that crevice, with Amos at the sweep and me at the oars, and as the river took us we saw that at the lower end of the canyon it dropped in a three-foot fall. That's not much, but it's enough to spell disaster if a boat turns sidewise.

We swept down the canyon, slid over the drop and into a whirlpool thirty feet across.

There were strange forces at work there in the depths of the river. The whirlpool was the center of a huge eddy, and as we spun into it I saw that it was saucer shaped, with the water being pulled down at the vortex with a loud, ominous sucking sound. Then suddenly that vortex started to boil up instead, as if the saucer were overflowing. It rose higher and higher, spinning faster and faster, lifting the boat with it.

Unless we could get clear before the vortex began to suck downward again we'd be pulled down with it. Amos shouted for me to pull harder but the oars seemed to have no effect on the spinning motion of the boat. I shipped them, grabbed up one of our poles, and as we whirled close to the rock wall I jammed the pole against it and heaved with all my strength. That push and Amos's furious work with the sweep broke the grip of the whirlpool. We shot clear and went bouncing downstream. In that same instant I heard the terrifying sucking noise behind us and looked back to see the center of the whirlpool sinking rapidly like water in a bathtub when the drain plug is pulled.

It had been a close call.

The Dease let up on us after that. It widened and slackened, gravel bars split it into channels, tree-covered islands appeared, bearberry and wild strawberries and lupine made a riot of color in every open glade. As we rounded a bend we saw a long low gravel bar. Lining the edge along the upper end a dozen or more Canada geese stood preening themselves and talking away like some women's church missionary meeting. They showed no fear of the boat until we got to within a hundred feet or so, then they ran along the bar gaining speed in unison, until, like a plane taking off from a runway, they rose slowly into the air, beating their way downstream.

A rim of white water ahead warned us of the first canyon. Cautiously we pulled ashore and tied the boat, then walked downstream to investigate. It turned out to be wide, severe rapids caused by a ridge of bedrock thrusting up through the fast shallow water. Gaps in the ridge allowed the river to pour down in a dozen different places, each one making a four- to six-foot fall and creating its own whirlpools. We crossed above the rapids to the other side. Here we found a narrow channel close inshore and we figured we could line down. We made camp knowing that if we passed these rapids successfully, only two or three miles further downstream was another, far worse canyon.

During the short hours of darkness I woke thinking I heard the boat scraping on the rocks. I sat up in my sleeping bag and looked down to the boat a hundred feet away. A large grizzly, probably attracted by the scent of bacon, was sniffing the boxes in the boat; the hump between his shoulders stuck high above his head, which was now hidden inside the boat. Reaching for my gun, I called Amos softly, then sent a shot over the bear's back, hoping that he wouldn't hurt the boat. He rolled back on his hind legs so fast that I thought I had accidentally hit or scraped him with the bullet. Then to our relief he took off at a rolling gallop downstream and into the brush. I gave up trying to sleep, half

Dease River scenery.

fearing that the grizzly would return and perhaps mistake me for a slab of bacon.

Lining the boat down between the rocks was a lot easier than we had expected although we both got soaked. Soon we were again sweeping out into the broad, easy channel below. The sun was already high and warm, the birds were singing, and a brightly plumed kingfisher swooped past us, dipped down, then turned upstream again, displaying all its brilliant colors as it flashed in the sun.

I rowed at a leisurely pace while Amos idled at the sweep, until, rounding another bend, we heard the roar of the canyon. Almost at the same instant we saw the huge foaming whitecaps tossing spray ten feet into the air as they bounced off a sheer rock wall on our side of the river. Across the river, rocks were strewn all the way to the far shore, but the water near the far bank looked calmer. Amos shouted above the din for me to pull over and try for the other side. Meanwhile he labored on the big sweep as we turned. We feared we could not make it across the massive current, for the momentum of the current increased and swept us closer to the rock-strewn whitecaps. When we did make it, we found the current so swift and shallow that we bounced on smaller rocks. I leaped out, bowline in hand. For a moment I was swept off my feet, then found footing between boulders and held the line tight as the boat swung in toward shore. Amos took the stern line and I held the bowline snubbed short. Slipping and slithering, every few yards dropping over our heads into a deep pool, we finally managed to line the load through. In an hour we were in calm water again, drifting toward the mouth of the river. The *Come What May* had shown its true colors. Though battered and bruised, the green spruce showed no sign of a crack.

The whole country now became a huge flat. We could see no mountains in any direction as we came to the mouth of the Dease and saw the wide sweep of the great Liard River. We saw the old log buildings of the Lower Post on the high bank across the Liard a half mile upstream.

The Indian population at the post, about fifty children and adults, stood at the top of the bank and watched us land. They looked more primitive than any Indians I had seen, some of them in worn skin clothing. It was plain that white men were an uncommon sight here.

We camped at the post for two days, trying to learn more of the rivers that lay ahead of us, the Frances and upper Liard. But no one could help us. We were told only that there was very dangerous water in the latter and we knew we would have to fight our way through it against the current. As for the Frances, nothing was known of it. We could not even find out how far it was to Frances Lake.

The Liard downstream from the Lower Post was fairly well known, although the trader told us that in all the years since the post was established only twenty-two white men, apart from Hudson's Bay Company employees, had ever come up the river to it. And what we were told about the Liard downstream only led us to expect trouble in the opposite direction.

Lower Post lay almost on the British Columbia–Yukon border, not far from where the Alaska Highway now passes Watson Lake. For a hundred fifty miles downstream it was a succession of canyons, savage rapids, and whirlpools, the trader said. Over the years whole boatloads of Hudson's Bay voyageurs had been lost in their treacherous waters, many of which had been given names that reflected their grim history. There were the Rapids of the Drowned, Whirlpool Rapids, Rivier de Vent Rapids, and Hell's Gate. The lower Liard had become a river of legend and terror, but nobody at the post could tell us what it was like upstream.

Then, on the second day we were there, a visitor arrived unexpectedly. He was a big, rollicking Swede and he had come down the Liard in a wonderful dugout canoe, hewed from the trunk of a cottonwood tree. It was thirty-two feet long and only about eighteen inches wide in the center, long and slim as a knifeblade. Its owner could turn that long canoe on a dime and send it skimming across the river like a water beetle. He knew more about the Liard upstream than anyone we had encountered and we invited him to share our evening meal.

A bad canyon, ten miles long, began six miles above the post, he said. In high water it was impassable. Even now, when the river was well below flood stage, he did not think we could pole upstream through it. And once we had entered it, there would be no way of getting out until we reached the head. The Swede strongly advised us to abandon our boat at this point and walk overland.

As for the Frances, he had not been on it but what he had heard about it from the Indians was all bad. Again, he thought we would be better off on foot. But our outfit was too heavy for that. Win or lose, we'd have to stay on the rivers.

We had another surprise visitor the last evening we were at the post. A fifteen-year-old Indian girl came to us. Her name, as near as I could make out, was Udzi and she wanted to travel with us to Frances Lake. She could cook and mend clothes, she said, and she was a good moccasin maker.

It was a request that would have tempted many men, for she was cleaner than most and attractive, with long black hair and a happy smile. And we knew we could assume that if we took her along she would come as the klooch of one or the other of us.

But that was not an arrangement that either Amos or I was interested in, and we sent her away, very disappointed.

8

THE TERRIBLE CANYONS

We are hard as cats to kill,
And our hearts are reckless still,
And we've danced with death a dozen times or so.
—"The Rhyme of the Restless Ones"

If I live to be a hundred I'll never forget the canyons on the Liard and the Frances.

Amos and I pushed out into the Liard at daylight. It was a big river here, close to a thousand feet wide, but the current was gentle except in the riffles and there were few places where our poles could not find bottom in seven feet of water. We rounded a bend and the high benches on the bank shut out the sight of Lower Post. So far as we knew we would see no other sign of civilization and no other white man until we came back this way in the fall—assuming we lived to come back. I was beginning to wonder about that.

We poled steadily, keeping to the inside of bends, where the current ran slowest. This was my first experience at poling upstream, but I was not long mastering it.

Amos took the stern pole and did the steering. My job in the bow was mainly to supply power, and there were a few rules that had to be followed. If I set the pole at an angle too far out from the boat we were swung sidewise in the current. If I let the pole slant under the boat, it was promptly torn from my hands, or if I hung on and tried to wrest it free I was dumped overboard with a splash. That happened twice the first morning and both times Amos roared with laughter at my dunking. The whole secret was smooth poling, and watching Amos it seemed almost effortless. But I noticed that sweat poured off him in rivulets under the hot sun of mid-July, and it was plain that he was working as hard as I was.

Six miles upstream from the post we rounded a bend and saw a line of white-crested, tumbling waves breaking the surface of the river ahead. We were approaching the lower end of the canyon.

We lined up through the first barrier of fast water, wading waist-deep close to the bank. We turned another bend and ahead of us sheer rock walls narrowed into the canyon itself and a dull roar like distant thunder told us what to expect. There is a strange quality about the sound of rapids, a pulsing rhythm that breaks their deep-throated muttering, born of the surge and ebb of heavy water tumbling and pounding against rocks. It was a sound both Amos and I knew well, and by its tone and volume we could gauge the speed of the Liard through the canyon.

We found a bit of good beach, tied our boat, and made lunch. That proved to be the last place where we could get ashore for four savage miles.

As we made the first turn above the lunch camp the bare rock walls rose sheer for three hundred to four hundred feet. Huge boulders and chunks of mountain stuck out of the water twenty and thirty feet high, scattered haphazardly between the walls, like half-submerged houses. The river boiled around and between these massive boulders, throwing waves eight and ten feet high and pouring down between them in cascades impossible for any boat to ascend.

It was straight poling now. There was no beach at all and in places the potholes were so deep that frequently we lost bottom with our poles. The power of the water tore at us, trying to sweep us against the rocks. The boat, of which we had been so proud, looked suddenly awfully small and puny. When a wave struck, tearing my pole from its grip on the river bottom, Amos would plunge his pole down firmly to hold the boat until I regained control.

Another slight bend in the river caused the main current to throw the full blast of water against a sheer wall on our side. We could not pole against the power of that water, smashing against the rock wall and shearing off in great sheets and waves as it tumbled downstream. The whole width of river here held huge boulders, making varying depths of wave-tossed boiling fury. We simply had to cross over and hope for a passage upstream on the other side. Gingerly we pushed to the lee of a huge boulder, being careful not to get sucked into its eddy. Downstream, it looked clear for about five hundred feet, which might give us time to make the far shore.

With a heave on our poles we shot out into the foaming torrent. Almost instantly the force of the water slapped the bow harder than we had anticipated and swung the boat almost half around. Lunging our poles down again and again, we found we were safely quartering toward the far bank, but facing downstream instead of up. Kneeling now on the dunnage, I leaned all my weight on the pole, pushing with every ounce of strength toward the other shore. Despite our efforts we were being carried swiftly downstream and suddenly the next string of rocks loomed close, sending spray high into the air. We must have been but thirty feet from the far shore when Amos struck a rock with the sweep, and was thrown off-balance for just a moment.

That moment was too long.

By luck we swung straight downstream, not sideways. The surge of current sucked us between two enormous boulders and we slid down the chute between them like a toboggan on a steep slope. In five minutes we were back at the lunch camp and pulling the boat ashore. In those five minutes we had lost our five hours of gain! All that terrific toil and sweat and risk, only to end up where we had started.

Yet perhaps we were lucky. We had learned that we

could get upstream the way we had come down, except for the twin boulders, and we felt sure we could keep to the shoreside of them. Tired and hungry, we settled down to a restful campfire, found a level spot for our bedrolls, and hung our clothes on nearby trees to dry out.

As the sun broke over the rim of the canyon we poled out into the river again. We made it to just below the perilous chute and found a narrow channel against the shore allowing us to proceed until we came to a jutting point that blocked all passage. We had to tie up and unload, and everything from the boat had to be carried up and over that point of rock. This was doubly tough because the rocks sloped like a church roof and the spray kept it wet and slippery. With the lightened boat floating high, I scrambled ahead of the point with the bowline in hand. Amos stood on the sharp point of rock and I feared that he might slip into the maelstrom below as he pulled on the stern line to keep the boat out in stream. It swamped in spite of our guiding, but somehow we lugged it half up the upper end of the rocky slope and bailed it out.

Reloading, we had to cross to the east side again, not far above our turning point of the day before. We struck hard against the rock wall on the far side, which here had a ten-foot overhang. The water almost immediately deepened so that we lost bottom on our poles. It would be suicide to try to cross again near here. In desperation I laid the pole in the boat and grabbed the overhanging rock wall with my fingers. To my surprise I found I could hang onto it and pull without my fingers slipping. Amos held his pole against the bottom although his arm was almost underwater, while slowly I literally clawed our way upstream for over an hour. It was grueling work. When we finally reached another eddy behind a point of rock, I jumped out onto the sloping rock surface and held the boat. Again we resorted to portaging. This time we were able to line the boat far enough out from the rock to avoid swamping.

We could now see the head of the canyon. The last mile was not nearly so rough and at sundown we cleared the head of the canyon and came to open country. With a sigh of relief and muscles that cried sorely for rest we made camp a mile above the last whitecaps. We felt we had bested the worst that the Liard had to offer.

Thereafter the river became a delight to travel on. Long sweeping bars allowed easy lining, the quietness and peace of the land soothed our tired bodies as we toiled upstream twelve hours a day.

Filling a kettle with water for supper at the river's edge one evening, I picked up a very heavy, shiny piece of rock. It proved to be silver-lead ore. While Amos cooked supper I took a prospector's pick and found a four-foot boulder of the same ore and then, where a recent landslide had scoured away the trees and gravel bank, I saw the vein from which the pieces had come. It was an exciting discovery, and I hurried back to Amos.

"I've located the vein," I told him. "It's four feet wide and streaked with this stuff."

Amos looked up from his cup of tea as casually as if I had found a dead fish. He studied the samples a minute, then growled, "No goddamn mining company is going to be interested in a find like this; it would have to run hundreds of ounces of silver to the ton to be any good in this god-forsaken wilderness." He was grouchy and discouraging. I think he was still overtired from the hardship of the canyon.

This country of the Liard River valley was as wild and naturally beautiful as any in the North. Wildflowers grew in abundance, mixing their perfume with that of the acres of wild roses blooming along the shores. Whiskeyjacks stole bacon from our frypan. Cow moose and their calves became more frequent, standing quietly in the slack water near shore and watching us undisturbed as we poled past. There were beaver houses in the sloughs and once we saw a pair of beaver cutting a poplar on the bank. They kept on working as if boats were an everyday event, and from their behavior and that of the moose we concluded that these animals had never seen a human before.

As we progressed the next few days the Liard widened and the current again slackened. Islands appeared, splitting the river into several channels in places, whereas the low-cut bank on the east shore showed the gravel to be almost entirely composed of quartz pebbles. At noon we tested a few pans for gold but found little to encourage us. The pans always showed a few tiny flakes, but such light gold we knew could be carried for miles in high water when the stream was yellow with muck and had a high density.

The world and its worries seemed very far distant. Here nature was in its raw state, unspoiled, untouched by man. Only at the mouths of the creeks was there any sign of even temporary habitation, and then only a few ax marks or small stumps, showing where some Indians traveling, or a trapper on his way to the post, had stopped to make a lunch fire or an overnight stop.

Once a kingfisher glided past us within a few feet of our heads. The bright blue flash went downstream a few hundred feet, then banked and turned, flying upstream past our camp again. The beautiful bird seemed to float on air as he glided swiftly over the water's surface, hardly moving his wings. He made a fast turn near the upper end of the bar, with chicken hawk suddenly dropping down out of the blue, almost on top of him. With a rough harsh screech, rather like the noise made by a suddenly whirled wooden noisemaker, the kingfisher changed course so rapidly that for a moment I lost sight of him. He headed toward the bank of trees, then, when almost at the timber's edge, turned again so swiftly that the pursuing hawk overshot him. Then the hawk, executing a graceful arc, soared upward above tree height and coasted along above the kingfisher at that level for several seconds. In and out they flashed, both fast flying.

It was indeed a joy to watch as they made sharp turns to right or left, or shot vertically upward, only to turn again and drop from a height of perhaps two hundred feet. Always the hawk *almost* struck the kingfisher, then on some flights the brilliant blue seemed to be chasing the brown pointed wings. I watched them, fascinated for a full ten minutes.

Then, as suddenly as he had come, the hawk disappeared, and the beautiful kingfisher flew to a dead tree overhanging the riverbank a few hundred feet downstream. There he froze in this position, watching the water beneath him for fish, his tousled topknot silhouetted against the smooth water downstream.

There were flocks of geese on the sandbars, walking ahead of us, taking flight only when we were almost on them, and at one of our overnight stops we watched a black bear and her two cubs plod down to the far bank of the creek where we were camped. The old bear could hardly have failed to notice our supper fire and the two men sitting beside it, but she paid no attention.

The cubs sat down on their fat little rumps close to the water and she waded in, her head lowered, watching intently for a fish. There was a sudden splash and a paw swipe too fast for the eye to follow, and a trout went sailing through the air and landed in the wild grass four or five steps back from the creek.

The two cubs pounced on it, growling and squealing like small pigs. One grabbed the head, the other the tail, and the noise subsided as they began to eat toward one another. What would have happened when they met I have no idea. Before we had a chance to find out the old bear cuffed a second fish in their direction. Immediately they dropped the fish they had and went to the new one.

As we moved up the Liard I was reminded more and more often of my feeling that the Garden of Eden must once have been this kind of place, with fear unknown.

The Liard widened and travel continued easy. We found chunks of lignite on the gravel bars, and even burned it in the place of wood for our campfires. It did an exceptional job of keeping away the swarms of mosquitoes that attacked us with the onset of the short nights.

At noon of the sixth day after leaving the Lower Post we came to the mouth of the Frances. A big timbered island split it into two channels. We picked the deeper one and floated into the river itself. It was warmer than the Liard, showing that it headed in lakes, and the current ran only three miles an hour. That first afternoon we even allowed

ourselves the luxury of hoping that the stories we had heard
of the upstream canyons were exaggerated.

We went for a swim that evening, enjoying the warmer
water, washed our clothes, and then sat down to mend
them. The hard travel on the Liard had taken its toll of
shirts and pants and jackets, and I even found myself wondering whether it might not have been a good idea to bring
the pretty little Indian girl along, after all.

The Frances and its creeks teemed with big grayling.
We put out a couple of set lines baited with rabbit kidneys
that evening and caught all the fish we needed in a very
short time. I had heard stories of explorers and prospectors
who had come close to starvation in this country. Taking the
abundance of fish into account, I still find that hard to
understand.

The next day the river narrowed, running between high
terraces, and the current turned fast. We made slow headway against it, and when we stopped for lunch the second
day we could hear a telltale intermittent roar coming from
upstream. We'd soon know what the canyons of the Frances
were like.

At sundown we came around a bend and a steep, rock-
strewn hell of white water stretched ahead of us as far as
we could see. We made camp and walked upstream to size
things up.

Broken limestone walls rose three hundred feet above
the river on both banks. Huge chunks had fallen away and
lay in a jumble in the riverbed, creating one ten-foot wave
after another. When we climbed to the top of the wall we
saw that this was not so much a rapids as a series of waterfalls, the lowest six feet high, where the river tumbled over
successive tiers of bedrock. The whole stretch as far as we
could see upstream sloped like a giant chute, and between
falls it smashed and roared with incredible force, shattering
itself against the great limestone boulders. No living man
could pole a boat upstream against its power and fury.
Unless we could find a way to line, along one bank or the
other, our boat journey was ended.

We named the place White Hell Canyon.

Our name was never recorded and did not stick. On maps today it is called Middle Canyon. But I still think ours was a far more appropriate name.

As we drank our tea by the fire that night, Amos suggested for the first time that we give up and turn back while we had whole skins. I thought for a minute he was testing me, and I laughed at him.

Standing on the wall above the river earlier, watching the roaring tumult of water and listening to the gurgling, sucking noise at the vortex of a huge eddy that whirled at our feet, I confess I had been frightened, and even found myself wondering whether if we challenged this canyon we would come out alive. But now I had my confidence back. There had to be a way through. I know now, almost fifty years later, that it was not courage but ignorance that influenced me. I simply did not know how to measure the terrible danger those falls and rapids posed for a boat.

I had learned to swim not long after I learned to walk, and now, after more than two years on the trails and rivers, I was hard as iron. But it was not my strength or swimming ability I was counting on, for I knew that no swimmer on earth would stand a chance in those chutes and eddies. The river would break every bone in his body before it released him. I was leaning on a confidence born of youth and inexperience.

Suddenly I sensed that Amos was dead serious about turning back. I saw that my laughing had offended him and I choked it off and fell silent. The disappointment of giving up when we were so close to our goal was almost too much to bear, and I opened my mouth to urge that if we had to quit the river we should fashion backpacks and go overland as the Indians did. But I thought better of it, knowing that whatever happened the decision lay in the hands of my partner. Tired as I was, I slept fitfully that night, wondering what that decision would be.

By morning Amos had forgiven what he thought was ridicule on my part. We scouted the opposite side of the canyon and concluded that we could line up to a point where a sloping shelf of rock ran down into the water. The wall here was of broken rock that had some brush and timber, and we could see a chance to portage our boat and outfit upstream for a thousand yards. That would take us to a place where we could line once more. It would be an almost unbelievable task, but there was no other way.

We left our camp pitched, and left our rifles, an ax, and some food behind in case of mishap. We lined the boat up to the rock shelf and went at the job of clearing brush and trees and building a roadway. The boat was far too heavy for two men to carry. The bigger trees we laid down for rails, clearing away the rocks and stumps between them. The smaller ones we cut into six-foot lengths for rollers. We would roll and skid the boat a thousand yards on those rails. We ran into an unforeseen barrier at the upstream end of our roadway, a sheer-walled ridge that went almost straight up for fifteen feet and then dropped the same distance to the river on the other side. But luckily we had brought along block-and-tackle gear and three hundred feet of line, and we thought we could manage the ridge.

The boat rolled reasonably well as long as the rollers stayed square across the crude rails. But that wasn't always the case, and we spent a good share of our time heaving the heavy boat back on the track. As one roller freed itself at the stern we carried it ahead and placed it under the bow, and as often as a rail was cleared we moved it to the head of the track. It was slow and grueling work and it took us two days to get the boat to the foot of the rock ridge. I have no words to describe the torture mosquitoes inflicted on us for those two days. We went back for our gear and supplies, portaged everything up to that point, rested and ate supper and went at the part of the job we dreaded most, skidding the boat up and over the ridge. We hung our two blocks to a stout tree, made a sling around the bow, got rollers in place, and the rest was surprisingly easy.

The roar of the river was like a passing freight train all that night, but neither of us heard it. We slept the sleep of utter exhaustion.

The sun slanted into the canyon at four o'clock the next

morning, rousing us. Amos fried grayling for breakfast while I loaded the boat, and we went back to lining. A short distance upstream the beach disappeared in a sheer rock wall a hundred feet high, which then gave way to a steep slope. I was able to walk along the top of the wall and haul on the bowline. Part of the time I could not even see the boat, hugging the base of the cliff below me. Amos stayed in it, fending it away from the rock wall with his pole.

I came to a deep gully that cut through the rim. It was only a few feet wide and I decided I could jump across. But as I gathered up a few extra feet of line and crouched for the jump my footing gave way beneath me. I slid half my own length, and then I was hurtling through a hundred feet of empty space, down to the river.

I struck with a huge splash and struck out furiously for shore, but the current swept me out toward midstream in spite of all I could do. I was carried swiftly past the boat and on toward a reach of savage water below. I swam desperately but it did no good.

It was a stroke of luck that saved me. I still had the bowline in one hand, and Amost was holding the boat against the raging current with his pole thrust hard against the bottom. He braced himself and hung on, and when I reached the end of my line I was brought up with a terrific jerk and swung in to the bank as if on a long pendulum. It had been a close call and Amos told me afterward that he had not thought I stood a chance.

We rested and I got my breath back, and then we decided that although the water here still ran swift and deep, we could go back to poling. We lined where we could, poled where there was no shore to walk on, and after another mile the rapids turned less savage and the going got easier. Then the current slackened suddenly, and there was no more white water in sight upstream. White Hell Canyon was behind us. But I understood fully now the stories we had heard of men who had disappeared in this wilderness and never been heard of again. Never again would such tales hold any mystery for me. I had come too close to being the subject of one.

Amos rests during our portage around the White Hell Canyon on the Frances River.

Amos had told me earlier that the Indians of this region did not travel the rivers. They preferred to go overland, on foot. I saw the reasons now. To begin with, they were not canoemen. Few of them could swim and river travel was not to their liking. And these rivers were too savage and danger- ous to serve as canoe routes.

Ten miles above the canyon, to our puzzlement, we smelled wood smoke drifting downstream on the wind. A little later we saw the stumps of trees on the bank and then a small cabin came into view. Dogs set up a howling and dark-skinned youngsters came running down to the shore to stare at us. We beached the boat and tied up, to be greeted by an old-time trapper named Watson. He was living here with his Indian wife and their children. Amos and I could hardly have been more surprised. Finding a white man on this remote and untraveled river was the last thing we had been led to expect.

The cabin was clean and reflected plainly the life-style of its occupants. Fishnets, snowshoes, and mooseskins were everywhere and a high cache stood close by the door. I still remember the wildflowers that were blooming in profusion on the dirt roof of the cabin.

Watson trapped down the Frances and the Liard as far as Fish Lake, at the head of the canyon about fifteen miles above Lower Post, he told us. Later he moved his residence to Fish Lake, and it became known as Watson Lake, the name it still carries. Today it is a major station on the Alaska Highway, and also the site of an important airport. That same highway runs within fifteen hundred feet of the canyon on the Liard where Amos and I had such a difficult time, but very few of the people who drive the road are aware that the canyon is there.

Watson knew the reaches of river he trapped, downstream from his cabin, but he could tell us almost nothing about what lay upstream. He said we would come to another canyon about seventy miles ahead but he did not know what it was like. As for Frances Lake, he could say only that about a dozen Indian families lived and trapped there, and there was an Indian trail leading overland through the mountains from the lake to Lower Post. Beyond that meager information, we'd be heading into the unknown again.

We began now to catch glimpses of distant mountains ahead, the first we had seen since leaving the upper canyon on the Dease. Far to the northeast the shining snow peaks of the Too-tscho Range pierced the sky and off to the east the lower ramparts of the Tses-i-tu Mountains showed now and then through openings in the timber. Game was plentiful, and the tracks of mink, fisher and otter showed everywhere along the river shore. Hardly an hour passed that we did not see beavers or muskrats or moose, and coyotes barked at us from the hilltops.

I fell 100 feet from the cliff at left center while attempting to line the *Come What May* around the rapids below.

Two days' travel above Watson's place brought us to a place known now as False Canyon. The old trapper had told us nothing about it. The river was fast, but the rapids offered no difficulty and we poled through them easily enough. We were nineteen days from the head of Dease Lake now, and although we could not be sure of the distance yet to travel, we thought we would reach Frances Lake in another week. One thing we were sure of. The canyon Watson had warned us about lay not far ahead.

When we reached it, it proved easier than those that lay behind us. There was a series of low falls that forced us to make three or four short portages of everything, including the boat, and in places the river ran too swift for poling. But we lined and carried, swamped and dumped the water out, resorted to block and tackle on one rock face, and made it through without risking our necks. After the furious water we had already seen, this place seemed almost tame.

Forty miles upstream islands began to fill the wide

The Hudson's Bay Company's Lower Post at the junction of the Dease and Liard rivers.

channel of the river. Geese rose frequently from the beaches, circling and alighting again before we were out of sight. We camped among the islands for two nights and each morning the clamor of geese awakened us at the first streak of daylight.

Now, far ahead, we could see that a wide valley opened out, hemmed in by mountains on both sides, and we were sure that Frances Lake lay in that valley.

The current slackened now. Every glade was filled with millions of wildflowers, while between the stands of cold-stunted trees heavy patches of red and black currants grew in profusion.

That night as we lay in our bedrolls close to the dying embers of campfire, excitement throbbed through me. Something special seemed to be waiting for me in this unmapped, unexplored territory, some great event was hovering over this lake in the middle of the most isolated area left in North America. I had less than three years' experience in this North country, and already so much had happened. I wondered what new adventures would unfold at Frances Lake. I slept fitfully and woke at four, ready to go.

The sun shone clear on a cloudless sky as we dug our poles into the shallow stream for the last few miles. The wide opening between the mountains took definite shape, mounds of glacial moraine poked up through some of the terraces, and large glacial boulders became visible in the river channels. Toward midafternoon the mountains came fully into view as the gap in the trees widened. Then, suddenly the bright glint of the sun shone on a vast body of water, dazzling our eyes as we came to the head of the river, and the huge expanse of the lake spread out ahead of us. The river emptied the lake at the southwest corner, leaving a wide, flat area to the east of the river, while a high, crystalline limestone wall hemmed in the west beach of the lake. Snowcapped mountains rose to nine thousand feet east of the lake. A mile or so away we could see a sandspit, covered in timber, sticking out into the lake for a half mile, cutting off any view beyond.

A keen sense of relief and satisfaction flooded through me. We had made it. We had conquered the four-hundred-odd miles of the Dease, the Liard, and the Frances. We had survived the terrifying canyons and rapids.

I broke out the oars. Rowing close to shore we reveled in the absence of river current. We beached at the sandspit and tied up in the lee of a good stand of spruce. After unloading the boat and making camp I walked alone to the end of the sandspit and gazed at my surroundings.

My first full view of the lake overwhelmed me. The scent of the wild roses perfumed the air like some English garden, and the sun-drenched trees tempered it with the gentle scent of spruce and pine. The jagged array of snow-capped mountains reflected their own glory on the mirror waters of the lake. But the silence that filled the huge valley dominated all my senses, after the weeks of roar and echo of the river. An ecstatic peacefulness engulfed me. It was, for a moment, as if I had walked through the veil into another world where a million years were set aside, enabling me to see and feel something extraordinary not given to everyday man. For a moment I was transported out of this world, so that I was outside of my body *and could see myself standing there.*

Slowly I sauntered back to camp, reluctant to break the spell that had come over me. I don't think Amos had any sentiment left in him. When I spoke of the great beauty of the lake he grunted something about finding the Indians to lead us to the silver-lead veins.

9
GOLD!

In the early days we were just a few, and we hunted
and fished around,
Nor dreamt by our lonely campfires of the wealth that
lay under the ground.

—*"The Parson's Son"*

We rowed up Frances Lake at a leisurely pace, shooting a
grouse or rabbit or catching a trout for our meals, taking
time to bake a bannock at our evening camps, picking raspberries, gooseberries, and cranberries, building soft spruce-
twig beds, traveling in ease compared with the hard river
miles that lay behind.

A few miles above the head of the river the lake made
a sweeping turn to the west. We were to learn later that it
forked here into two arms, like a giant wishbone, with a
broad peninsula between. But the entrance to the east arm
was narrow and obscured by islands, so that unless you
rowed close enough to shore to feel the current, which was
strong here, it looked to be no more than a small bay. We
passed it without paying it any attention.

Ten or a dozen miles farther up the west arm we found
the first sign of human habitation. A bundle of long poles
stood stacked against a tree. They were winter tepee poles,
and there were the remains of many fires on the ground. The

99

poles had been cut at the height of a man's shoulders above the ground, indicating deep snow at the time. Plainly this was the site of a winter camp for the Frances Lake Indian families.

Late that afternoon, nearing the head of the lake, we saw the smoke of a campfire rising through the trees. We pulled to the beach and tied up. Here was journey's end. The fire was tiny, built between two tents. When we walked closer we saw that the tents were old and stained and that many holes had been burned in them. Squatted in front of the fire was the oldest Indian I had ever seen.

He wore nothing but a soiled knee-length shirt of caribou skin. His face, deep copper brown in color and as wrinkled as a prune, was half hidden behind matted white hair that hung down to his shoulders. From the way his rheumy old eyes searched for us as we stepped close, I sensed that he was half blind, and his bony arms hung in front of him as if helpless.

But it was his nails that were the strangest thing about him. I had never seen human nails like them. His scrawny hands ended in actual claws, about an inch long and curved like an eagle's. Below bony legs his feet were gnarled and misshapen, too, and the toenails were almost as curved and long as those on his fingers.

I walked up to him with my hand held high in greeting and tried him with "Clehahya!," the Chinook equivalent of "Hi, friend." When that evoked no reaction, I went to the Tahltan dialect with "Closh Tillicum." But he didn't understand that either. Nevertheless, he was obviously anxious to be friendly. He had been stirring the fire with a small stick, and he waved it excitedly and jabbered in a language I could not make out.

The tent beyond the fire had no one in it. Pieces of blanket and clothing, blackened pots, and old moccasins were strewn about. Then, inside the tent nearest me, I saw an old gray-haired woman sitting cross-legged on a pile of mooseskin, dressed in a faded cotton dress. After a minute she came out and stood beside the man. She did not seem to be quite as old as he was, but I assumed she was his wife.

I handed him my tobacco pouch. A grin spread across his wrinkled face and he fished out a pipe from a pile of rags behind him. The bowl was made from a piece of dry alder and the stem, about five inches long, was a bone from the penis of a grizzly bear. I had seen Indian pipes of that kind before. The woman went immediately back into her tent, and in a moment she came out with one like it. The two of them stuffed the small bowls with my tobacco and lighted them with a brand from the fire.

Next the man, talking steadily, interrupted himself long enough to reach for an empty pot and indicated in sign language that he wanted a drink. I took the pot to the edge of the lake, filled it, and hung it on a stick over the fire.

I knew little about sign language but I fell back on it now, first asking where the occupants of the other tent were. He seemed to understand. He circled a bony arm to indicate a day's travel, the sunup to sundown sign, and made it three times. They would be back in three days, I concluded.

The only food in the tent was a small chunk of dried moose meat. I made signs to indicate eating, and he grinned and pointed to the mountains to the west. I assumed the other Indians had gone hunting there to replenish the camp's food supply.

Finally Amos and I rowed away to make our camp beside a tiny creek a hundred yards down the lake. We'd wait here until the rest of the band returned from their hunt and then we'd try to locate the body of galena, the silver-lead ore we had come to find.

After supper we went back to the old Indian and his wife, gave them a half pound of tea and a plug of tobacco, and showed them a sample of the galena. The man understood instantly. He pointed across the lake to the east and made the sunup and sundown sign twice. We'd find the ore there, two days back in the mountains.

The next day Amos and I declared a holiday. We washed and mended our clothing, scoured our pots and pans with sand, set out a fishline, and cleaned and oiled our guns. Finally we went for a swim.

The day after that, to fill the time until the Indians

returned, we poled up toward the head of Frances Lake. We came to a mile-wide delta where a big river (we'd learn later it was the Finlayson) flowed in from the west, and to our surprise we found a white man's old cache still standing. There were two possible explanations of its origin. We knew that six men had spent the winter at Frances Lake during the gold rush of 1898. Either they had built it or it had been erected by the explorer Dr. G. M. Dawson in 1887. In either case, it had been well built and was in surprisingly good shape.

The Finlayson came down to Frances Lake through a canyon, and then cut through the big delta that it had laid down over the centuries. The delta almost filled the lake now, leaving a channel only a hundred feet wide between itself and the eastern shore, and the current of the upper six miles of the lake flowed swiftly through that channel. The river itself emptied leisurely into the lake close by.

We poled into the river and up through the delta to the canyon. The water was shallow and easily navigable for two or three miles. There the south wall had broken down in a half-moon flat of gravel benches and channels that carried water only when the river was at high stage. Upstream from that crescent-shaped flat the canyon walls pinched in and we could pole no farther.

We beached the boat and went ahead on foot. We had seen big quartz veins in the rock wall on the north side of the river, hinting at gold, and Amos chipped off samples with his prospector's pick. He walked ahead and I followed him with pick and shovel. His samples showed some mineralization but no free gold.

Across from these veins there was a gulley, slanting down from the rim of the canyon and cutting across the gravel flat to the river. At the bottom of it a tiny stream trickled in, hardly big enough to deserve the name of creek. At the mouth of that trickle, walking on exposed bedrock where the water was only a few inches deep, I saw something glint under my feet as if a small mirror had caught the sun. I was a couple of steps past it before the significance of that flash registered. I stepped back, then moved slowly forward, and the gleam of a gold nugget leaped at me through three inches of water.

"Gold, Amos!" I shouted. "I've found a nugget!"

I dropped to my knees in the shallow water and tried with my belt knife to dig it out of the crevice where it was wedged. Mud roiled the water and I lost sight of the precious nugget. I hacked into the crevice upstream with the pick and waited for the water to clear. When that happened the current had moved the small lump of gold and I could no longer see it.

I ran for the gold pan in the boat. Amos watched me a bit skeptically as I cleared the crevice of mud and rock and filled the pan. Crouching beside a deeper channel, I washed that pan of dirt very carefully. My nugget flashed at me again the first time I tilted the pan, and when I finished, a string of specks and small nuggets lay like a shining halo bordering the residue of black sand left in the bottom of the pan.

I had discovered gold!

On a nameless creek, in what seemed at that moment a place a million miles from civilization, the dream of every prospector had come true for me. I had found the eternal treasure.

I do not believe that any man to whom that has happened can tell others what the feeling is like. Unless you have made a strike you cannot understand the magic of the words. An old-timer once told me that when it happened to him his heart started to pound and he felt the hair rise on the nape of his neck as if a grizzly had poked its head out of the brush and looked him in the eye at arm's length. For me it was as if a cord that had been tied around my heart had suddenly been broken.

I have marveled countless times since at the strange way our lives hang on some small accident of fate. Had that little nugget been covered with a quarter inch of sand, my whole future would have been utterly different.

Amos and I dug and panned until dusk, possessed by gold madness, forgetful of everything around us save the gravel and mud and the flakes and small nuggets we found.

Not a single pan failed to show color, and when we went to the boat and started back to camp, in three hours' time we had recovered half an ounce of gold, worth $10, with a single pick and pan. Good panning, that!

The Indians were late in getting back from their hunt but we didn't mind the delay. The next four days went by like a dream. We were up at dawn each morning, wolfing down a hurried breakfast and rushing back to what we were calling the Half-Moon Discovery, with pick and shovel and pan.

We tested many places in that half-mile-long crescent of gravel and there was gold wherever we looked. There was not a day that did not yield at least half an ounce, and if we could take out that much using a pan we knew we could do far better with a sluice box. We had made a truly rich strike, and there was enough of it to keep two men busy for years with pick and shovel. Working for the Hudson's Bay Company two summers before, I had been paid $125 a month and thought it good wages. Now, if we could rig a sluice box we could each make that much in two days.

We had not brought the whipsaw with us, and so had no way to fashion lumber for a sluice box. But for now that could wait. Even if we could persuade the Indians to work for us when the time came, it would take many summers to work the Half-Moon clean.

The fourth day the Indian hunters came back. They were waiting for us when we returned to camp that evening. Little Jimmy, who had shown Amos the galena sample back at Telegraph Creek, was in the group. He told us that he had started back to Frances Lake overland as soon as he left us there, and he had made better time afoot than we had by boat. With him were two other Indian men, Chief Smith and Caesar. I decided that the party of stampeders who had wintered at Frances Lake in 1898 had named them. Little Jimmy apparently had come by his name from the trader at Lower Post on the Liard.

All three of the men spoke broken English, so our language troubles were at an end. They told us they had had a good hunt. They had cached part of their moose meat and they returned to the camp with sixteen pack dogs each carrying forty pounds. Nobody would be short of food the remainder of the summer.

The three cleared up for us the identity of the old Indian with the eagle-claw nails. He was Dentiah, they said, an Indian word for "Old Chief." Chief Smith was a de-scendant of his, but we could not be sure which generation. In any case, the old man's age was hard to believe. We learned that he and his son had helped to build the trading post at Pelly Banks, built by Robert Campbell for the Hudson's Bay Company in 1842. Since he had a son old enough at that time to be hired for heavy work, it seemed likely that the old man had been born shortly after 1800. That meant he was now about 123 years old. He died at Frances Lake in 1929, claiming to be 127. He was probably close to right.

After supper that evening the Indians visited our camp for gifts. We gave them tea and tobacco, the two luxuries they prized most, and when that ceremony was over all of the families save Chief Smith's left, walking the beach to the mouth of the Finlayson. They waded across the river, and where the lake was narrowest between the delta and the east shore they pulled a mooseskin boat down from a high cache, climbed into it, and the entire group paddled across to the east side of the lake in two trips.

Chief Smith and his fine-looking young wife and children occupied the tent that stood beside the Old Chief's.

Half-a-dozen campfires glowed on a hill on the east shore of the lake that night, and strange singing drifted to us across the water, much like the lilting, half-key songs I had heard among the Tahltan Indians. Dogs from that camp started to howl, the dogs on our side of the lake replied, and the eerie savage chorus continued without letup for more than an hour. The North has no sound that speaks more eloquently of its wilderness and solitude.

Amos and I made arrangements with Little Jimmy and Caesar to go at once for a look at the silver-lead ore. From

Caesar with his squaw and child on the West Arm of Frances Lake.

Caesar we learned that Frances Lake had two arms. We would row down the west arm, part way up the east, leave the boat, and hike into the mountains on foot.

I left our camp early the next morning to collect our tools at Half-Moon, while Amos made ready for the trip. When I got back, the whole Indian encampment was paying us a ceremonial visit.

Two more men, Jules and Meegan, had shown up with their families, making a total of six men including the Old Chief. There were five or six women and between thirty and forty kids of all ages. Not one of the women or youngsters had seen a white man before. The women were dressed in their finest, brightest clothes and the men wore cleaner clothing than usual. Caesar told me that there were two more men who belonged with the group, but they were off trading for salt, traps, and tea at Lower Post on the Liard. They had gone by way of the long mountain trail that followed the valley at the foot of the high slopes to the east, and they would return the same way, using log rafts to cross small streams. They were not expected back for another month.

Plainly these Indians were not canoe people. So far as I ever learned, none of them could swim and they rarely touched water except when they had to wade across a creek. But they had long ago mastered the technique of making remarkable and very serviceable skin boats of moose hide. The one this band used in crossing Frances Lake at the delta of the Finlayson was typical. About twelve feet long, it consisted of a light frame made from alder poles with three mooseskins stretched over it. The skins were sewed together while green, stretched in place as tight as a drumhead, laced with rawhide, and allowed to dry. They shrank as they dried, and the finished boat was as waterproof as any canoe. So light that one man could lift it over his head or raise it up to a cache without effort, the boat could carry a ton of meat and several people and still draw no more than a few inches of water. Empty, it rode the surface like a water spider. In a wind it was hard for one man to control, but apart from that it was a wonderful boat for hunting, fast and quiet, with no sound when waves slapped against the dried skins. On many occasions, using a wooden boat, I have known its noise to alert a moose. In the skin boat a hunter could drift almost on top of one without alarming it.

Since none of the Indian women or children had ever seen blond hair (mine was bleached almost white by the summer sun now) or blue eyes before, I was a focus of curiosity for the whole group. To one little girl about six years old, not quite as shy as the rest, I handed a piece of bannock spread with jam. She ran into the trees with it, but word of the treat spread and in minutes I was surrounded by a dozen laughing youngsters, their straight black hair flying in the wind. I set a can of jam and a whole bannock on the end of our camp table and told them, through Caesar, to share it. Even some of the women edged in and helped themselves, and when the bannock was gone there were a lot of sticky faces and some very wide grins.

At sunrise the next morning Little Jimmy, Caesar, Amos, and I left our camp in the *Come What May* for the trip to the deposit of galena ore. As we made our way down the west arm of Frances Lake the two Indians tried their hand at rowing, but apparently they had never before been in a wooden boat or handled oars, and the latter were too much for them, especially for Little Jimmy. He splashed with each stroke, drenching all four of us.

We stopped on an island for lunch, and in early afternoon we came to the narrows where the east arm entered the lake, confined between high banks, fast currented and island choked. We turned up against the current, and a hundred yards farther on a trail came down to the water. It ended at the top of the bank, where two decrepit log cabins still stood, near the original Fort Frances, abandoned by the Hudson's Bay Company in 1851 and never rebuilt. The Indians used those cabins in winter now, when they were trapping. Seventy-four years of aging and weathering had obliterated all trace of the trading post, but we searched

One of the mooseskin boats of the Frances Lake Indians.

and found the rotted ground logs of the main building, now
well overgrown, a few signs of other buildings, and a heavy
iron pot.

We camped there that night and started up the east
arm of the lake the next morning, alternately rowing and
lining against the current that drained the arm. A few miles
farther on we came in sight of high mountains that sloped
down to within a mile of the beach. Here the arm widened
into a broad sheet of water, and we rigged a sail from a
couple of blankets and our poles. The head of the lake
could be seen now through our binoculars, twenty miles
distant, ending in a timbered flat.

I have never in my life seen a lake of more entrancing
beauty than the east arm of Frances. It has never gained
renown, probably for the reason that so few men have
looked upon it, but it must surely rival the most beautiful
of the known lakes of the earth, with its timbered shores
and mountain reflections.

Ten miles short of the head of the arm we tied up at
the mouth of a small creek, ate lunch, and started on foot
for the galena veins.

A trail zigzagged up beside the creek, and we had
walked only a short distance when the Indians pulled up
and Caesar pointed to a place where the carpet of moss had
been scraped off the ground.

"Find um here," he said.

A vein of solid galena lay exposed, eighteen inches
wide, held between walls of black schist.

Caesar went on to tell us that he had been hunting
moose on a flat half a mile up the mountain, and had killed
a big one. Having no dogs along to pack out the meat, he
had made a sling of the hide, loaded it, and dragged and
skidded it down the slope through the thin brush that covered the hillside. At this place the load had pulled the moss
away and he had seen the galena ore.

We camped there for several days, exploring the area.
The Indian had made a find of considerable importance.
We uncovered ore all the way back to the beach, and the

The East Arm of Frances Lake.

vein widened as it dipped. Next we located an even wider vein farther up the creek.

The second day I climbed the highest ridge above us, and from its crest I could see all of Frances Lake and something like eighty miles in every direction. That was a sight I'll never forget.

We staked and cleared boundary lines for eight claims. That covered all the mineral showings that the company who had financed our trip could want. The job we had come so far to do was finished. Now we could go back to our gold panning.

We made a fast trip back to camp, and decided to make a crude sluice box from the trunk of a dead cottonwood. It was a stub about twenty feet tall, with the top broken off. We cut it and chipped away the rotted wood at the heart, leaving only the shell. In one day the job was done, and we skidded it across the gravel flat to the site of our diggings.

To bring running water into the sluice box, we built a rock wing-dam running out from shore into the Finlayson. Next we tore our boat sail into strips and I sewed them up with oversize stitches to form a crude canvas hose eighty feet long and six inches in diameter, held open at the upper end by a wooden frame. It provided a good flow of water into the head of the box. Then we went to work with the one shovel we had.

When we had washed all the gravel within reach of the box we used our boat to float more down, a yard at a time. At the end of two days we cleaned out the concentrate trapped in the bottom of the sluice box by pole cleats, and washed it in our gold pan. In those two days we had recovered more than fifty dollars' worth of gold. Our discovery was a true bonanza.

My partner and I agreed then and there on complete secrecy. When we returned to civilization we would report on the silver-lead veins we had come for, but the gold discovery would remain known only to the two of us.

10
LONG WINTER TRAIL

Let us probe the silent places, let us seek what luck
  betide us;
Let us journey to a lonely land I know.
There's a whisper on the night wind, there's a star
  agleam to guide us,
And the Wild is calling, calling—let us go.
                            —*"The Call of the Wild"*

With freeze-up time only six weeks away, Amos and I calculated very carefully how long we could continue our mining operation and still get out of the country before slush
ice formed in the rivers and trapped us for the winter.

Frost had whitened the ground night after night since
we staked the galena claims. The edge of our sluice box was
rimmed with ice each morning, the beach sand was frozen
hard, and pebbles at the edge of the river glistened like
jewels when the morning sun struck their sheath of ice.
Playing our mounting profits against the oncoming winter
was risky business, but we agreed to keep on mining as long
as we dared.

The rivers were at their low autumn levels now, and
the rapids would be far less difficult and dangerous than

113

they had been when we made our way into the country. On top of that, we'd be going downstream on the Frances and the Liard, and could make much better time. The trip out would take days less than the trip in.

We figured three days down the Frances, one down the Liard, then eight up the Dease to McDame Post, a total distance of one hundred and sixty miles. Seven more days to Porters Landing, a day to the head of Dease Lake, and a three-day hike over the trail to Telegraph Creek. Twenty-three days if luck was with us all the way. We'd cut it as thin as we dared, but to be safe we'd have to allow a month for the trip out.

The day came finally when we did not dare to tarry any longer. On September 16, my twenty-fifth birthday, we cleaned up the sluice box, panned the last of our gold, and stood the box against a tree. We'd head south right after daybreak the next morning, and we'd be taking out more than six hundred dollars' worth of dust and nuggets for seventeen days of hard work.

We loaded only the necessary things into the boat that night, leaving the rest of our outfit behind for me. I was coming back. With much bantering and many promises to the Indians, we pushed into the lake as soon as breakfast was finished, with Amos at the sweep and me at the oars.

We raised a blanket for a sail, and ran the length of Frances Lake and several miles down the Frances River that first day. Wedges of wild geese flew overhead all day long, driving steadily into the south, their distant flight talk drifting down to remind us that it was time to go. We counted seven of their V's in sight at one time. We slept in the open on the riverbank that night, and two inches of snow covered our bedrolls. Ice rimmed the boat and covered the poles and oars at daybreak, and my hands turned stiff with cold on the oar handles. The geese were right. It was indeed time to go.

We swept swiftly downstream, with Amos half idle at the sweep, and reached the first rapids the second day. The water was so low that they no longer looked dangerous. We made one short portage, lined through the worst places, and ran the green chutes where we could. The boat slid down them rather like skis on a steep slope.

False Canyon gave us no trouble, and at dusk that night we camped above the stretch we had named White Hell Canyon. Here again the river had lost much of its savage power, but it still had enough to compel us to make a portage of everything except the boat.

We soon came to the place where I had come so near to drowning on the way up. Here we pulled ashore to look things over.

Every hour counted now. We were at least sixteen or seventeen days from Dease Lake, and the threat of slush ice in the rivers hung over us like a sword blade. The rivers of the North country run heavy with such ice weeks before the lakes lose their summer heat and freeze over. The ice forms first in the small creeks, especially those that rise in the high mountains and are snow fed. It flows out into the river and more forms, and soon it becomes very difficult to run a boat downstream and totally impossible to fight upstream against the current. There is enough hard ice mixed with the slush to cut a boat to ribbons in a few miles. At best the margin of time left to us was very short.

We finally agreed that Amos would pack our outfit to the foot of the rapids and I would run them in the boat. I pushed the boat out into the stream and grabbed the oars.

Rowing like a madman in an endeavor to keep steerageway, the thrill leaped in me like a stab of pain as the tiny boat struck the first whitecaps. The force of the heaving masses of water carried the little boat like a matchbox, flinging it from one bouncing wave to the next. Snatching quick glances over my shoulder I saw the fury pouring over submerged rocks and channeled between others, the waves flattening out to pour down the chute and bouncing off both sides of the restricting rocks. The boat, as if held in the clutches of some demon of the river, swept through the chute and fell into the maelstrom of foam below. Somehow the impetus gained above carried the boat through the turmoil: it shot through and out of the spray, half filling the boat, and I found myself pulling hard in smooth fast water until I gained the shore below.

We reloaded the *Come What May*, rode the current of the Frances down to the wide-sweeping Liard, and camped that night at the head of the canyon on that river. Though this canyon was worse than those on the Frances, low water had tamed it; the thundering roar was gone, and there was not a single stretch too savage to run with the loaded boat. By midmorning we pulled to shore at the Lower Post, stocked up quickly on butter, bacon, and jam, and poled across the Liard and into the mouth of the Dease. The rest of the way to Dease Lake would be upstream. But wherever poling was difficult or too slow, the summer boat crews of the Hudson's Bay Company had cut a trail along one bank or the other. We took advantage of those trails, lined up through the Lower Canyon in dead low water, soon came to the Upper Canyon and passed it without difficulty. On the eighth day after leaving our camp on Frances Lake we were at the McDame Creek Post, four days ahead of the best schedule we had hoped for.

Here luck was with us. A mining crew was closing down for the winter. They'd be going up to Dease Lake in two more days, using a small scow powered by an outboard, and they invited us to join them. Our summer of hardship and danger was at an end.

We cached our boat, and the trip the rest of the way up the Dease on the scow was more fun than work. We had to pole a few times in fast water, but there were plenty of hands to do it and we made good time. We took four days to reach Porters Landing at the foot of Dease Lake, and another day took us to the lake's head. That night the thermometer fell to two below zero and the ice around the shore was thick enough to support a man. We had come out not a day too soon.

We rode from Dease Lake to Telegraph Creek on the last tractor train of the year. It was a three-day ride, much of it in a heavy snowstorm. When we reached Telegraph Creek the *Hazel B No. 2* was tied to the bank, ready to leave in the morning. Amos and I would go separate ways now. He was leaving for the Outside, where he had a wife and family. He had no desire to winter in that faraway wilderness. I traded him some other mining property I owned, farther south, for his share in the Frances Lake claim. I would go back to my gold discovery alone. I planned to stay there a year, living mostly off the country. That way I figured I'd be able to come south with a real stake.

Ice was forming along the river shores now, and old Ah Clem, the Chinaman and town weather prophet, pulled his fishnet out of the water where he had been gill-netting salmon all fall. Winter must be just around the corner.

The *Hazel B*, by the dawn's first light, cast off and slid silently downstream. I stood on the high bank overlooking the river and watched her go. There was always something so decisive about watching the last boat pull out.

The next few days I outfitted carefully, exercised my six dogs to run off some of the fat they had put on while boarding at the old Stikine Hotel.

To those who showed curiosity I showed samples of the galena ore. The advantage of the galena was that it supplied a cover and enabled me to keep my gold findings to myself.

In a few days I was ready. I went last of all to Harry Dodd, the Gold Commissioner, confided my secret and my plans to him and left my poke of gold with him for safe-keeping. Then I loaded forty-pound packs on each of my dogs, shouldered a heapy pack of my own, and faded quietly out of town. I was on my way back to the Half-Moon, but nobody in Telegraph Creek except Dodd knew that.

Temperatures were down around the zero mark. The trail was frozen hard and covered with light snow, neither deep enough for dogsled travel nor a hindrance to the loaded pack dogs. I carried some tools, including a six-foot crosscut saw, my .30/06 Winchester and a .22 Remington repeating rifle slung over my shoulder, and my down sleeping bag in the pack on my back. I did not yet have a tent.

The traveling was good, but I did not hurry and it took four days to make the seventy-five miles to the head of Dease Lake. The Hudson's Bay Company had a new post there now, a result of the gold discoveries and the inrush of prospectors and miners, and it had all the equipment I needed. I bought a toboggan, a lightweight silk tent, and a small stove with a cast iron top. I also bought picks, gold pans, two more shovels, a seven-foot whipsaw, a two-inch auger, and the other tools I would need. The auger I'd use to drill holes for wooden pegs that would hold together the logs of the cabin I intended to build, and it would also come' in handy for building rafts to carry the dogs and me across any unfrozen rivers or large creeks we might encounter.

From the Dease Lake Indians I purchased a few sacks of dried fish for the dogs and also for myself, in the event I was unable to get fresh meat or fish on the long sled trip, although I had few doubts on that score. I had left a gill net on the high cache at Frances Lake. Once there I knew I could rely on fresh fish, both for the team and for my own needs.

There was a shelf of ice along the shore of Dease Lake, thick enough for safe travel with the toboggan if we kept close to the beach. Light snow fell during the night I stayed at the post, which meant good going for the dogs. The temperature had dropped to fifteen below zero, and I felt confident that the Dease River would be frozen over by the time we reached it. I got to the head of the river the second day, found the ice firm and safe, and not enough snow to form bad drifts. Near rapids the ice was broken and rough, but by picking my way or falling back on the trail used by boat crews in summer, I had no difficulty.

At night I staked the dogs to separate trees, pitched a canvas fly for myself, and cut spruce boughs to keep my sleeping bag off the snow. I cooked my meals over an open fire, fed the dogs dried whitefish when I didn't shoot enough rabbits for them. Once I had a chance to kill a moose but passed it up, knowing the meat would make too heavy a load.

The Dease River is beautiful in winter, more so even

than in summer. The high mountains on either side reflected every shade of pink and white in their snow-covered slopes, and the spruce forests came right to the water's edge. Except for the swishing of the toboggan and the panting of the dogs the silence surrounded us so forcefully it made me feel somehow as if we were trespassing into some secret land, some forbidden paradise. I traveled from daylight to dusk with but a few minutes' rest for noon stop. A few times I came across a trapper's trail but did not see another human.

I made the hundred and eighty miles from the head of Dease Lake to Lower Post on the Liard in eight days. From the Indians at the post I bought a supply of babiche, moose rawhide thongs for spare snowshoe webbing. From them I also learned the location of the trail used by the Frances Lake Indians when they came to the post to trade. It followed close to the foothills east of the Frances River, they told me, thus missing the steep cuts made by creeks running into the Frances. The trail wound north and northwest, almost on a straight line to Frances Lake, a far more direct route than going up the Liard sixty miles to the Frances River and following that to the lake, as Amos and I had done.

One of the Indians went with me when I was ready to leave and showed me where it came down onto the flats of the Liard.

"Take trail here," he said. "Frances Lake up there," and he waved an arm to the north.

I put the dogs on the trail, left the Indian, and entered as beautiful a winter wonderland as I have ever seen. The snow lay everywhere, white and clean and deep, broken only by the occasional track of a moose, the packed trails of snowshoe rabbits, or the footprints of wolf and marten, fox and lynx. And all that white world was still with a silence unlike the quiet anywhere else on earth.

The winter stillness of the northern wilderness has a hushed quality all its own. On a windless day when a few flakes of snow eddy softly to the earth, or in the flooding brilliance of a moonlight night, that absence of sound presses down upon the mind and spirit so tangibly that it can be felt. But it brings peace, not loneliness. This was the perfect solitude I had come North to find, and I reveled in it.

Two days out from Lower Post we came on a moose yard, where fifteen or twenty of the big animals had gathered for the winter in heavy timber close to a big stand of willows. They had shelter and a food supply there and would stay in the yard until spring, keeping trails open to the willow flats by daily use.

It was an easy matter to pick out and kill a young bull, and that night the dogs had a feast of fresh moose. We laid over a day and rested, and I built a cache to hold the meat we could not carry. It would keep until spring, and if I needed to return to the post in an emergency during the winter, it would be there waiting for me. Under the right circumstances, that could mean the difference between life and death for a man traveling by himself in that vast wilderness.

The trail was not as smooth as river ice but it was cut out fairly well, although the Indians had followed their practice of going around rather than cutting through windfalls, so there were frequent sharp turnouts. Nevertheless we made steady time.

We were still several days from Frances Lake when, shortly before camping time one afternoon, the dogs started suddenly to sniff the air and pick up their pace. I knew we were approaching game of some kind. We rounded a turn in the trail and looked down on a small lake, and feeding on low brush along the shore was a band of some thirty barren-ground caribou, the first of their kind I had ever seen.

The dogs went frantic but I quieted them. For ten minutes I stood in the shelter of the timber and watched that feeding band. They were much smaller and more delicately made than the big woodland caribou I had seen in the mountains bordering the Dease River valley, with beautiful, finely shaped antlers; and they traveled in larger herds.

At that time they migrated south and east from the Arctic coast barrens in early winter, as soon as the ice in the rivers was strong enough to support them. Usually by

the end of November they had come as far as the headwaters of the Pelly River west of Frances Lake, and from
there a few bands, such as the one I was watching now,
wandered on into the Frances River valley. I believe that
was as far south as these barren-ground herds traveled. In
early spring they headed northwest again, crossing the
upper Yukon and drifting on across Alaska to their calving
grounds on the tundra. As civilization intruded on that vast
country, the caribou changed their habits.

The little band down in the willows was an entertaining
sight, feeding, then walking on, pawing away the snow or
using the shovel tine of their antlers to clear it from a bush
where they wanted to nibble. I could have killed one of them
easily enough, but we were still too far from our destination
to take the meat along. I was sure there would be other
caribou where we were going. But I chained my dogs very
securely that night, knowing what they would do if they
got loose.

High mountains on the far side of the Frances River
showed up more and more plainly now, and I could also
see the peaks that bordered the east arm of Frances Lake.
We were nearing journey's end. Game became more and
more plentiful, and then we found the first human sign we
had seen since leaving Lower Post, the snowshoe trail of an
Indian trapper.

I was sure he belonged to the band with whom Amos
and I had spent half the summer, but his trail did not go
toward Frances Lake, so we crossed it and kept going. An
hour before dusk we came down off a high ridge and the
lake lay before us, frozen out for half a mile along the shore,
filled with drifting ice in the middle. We crossed to the west
shore and I drove the dogs into a stand of heavy timber and
made camp. I was almost home.

I had enjoyed every mile of that long solitary trip, and
it had also done much to give me confidence in myself. I
had been two and a half years in the North now, and there
was very little resemblance left between the green cheechako who had gone up the Stikine to Telegraph Creek and

the seasoned, trail-hardened, self-reliant sourdough who mushed his dogs across the end of Frances Lake that cold winter afternoon.

I knew how to hunt game and catch fish to feed my dogs and myself, how to make a shelter on the trail, which ice was safe and which was not. I also knew the dangers of the rapids, the deadly threat of storms and of cold at fifty and sixty below. So long as I obeyed the laws of the wilderness and paid them the respect that was their due, I would be safe enough.

We traveled up Frances Lake all the next day on the rim ice, the dogs pulling steadily, and camped that night at the delta of the Big Sheep Lick River, the Il-es-tooa of the Indians. It was later named for me, and today's maps show it as Money Creek. I appreciate the honor but I like the old name better.

I had only five miles to go now to the campsite Amos and I had used, where I planned to build my cabin. I drove the dogs on to the place early the next morning. It was deserted. My Indian neighbors were gone to the last man, woman, and child, scattered on their trapping grounds. The stones around their fire rings were covered with snow and the tent poles were stacked against a tree.

I faced a winter of total solitude.

11
THE CHRISTMAS CARIBOU

Were you ever out in the Great Alone, when the moon
was awful clear,
And the icy mountains hemmed you in with a silence
you most could hear?
—"The Shooting of Dan McGrew"

I built a frame of light poles in the middle of a thick stand of spruce, pitched my silk tent over it, covered the floor with spruce boughs, and installed my little stove. Next I made a small table and low pole bunk. I stored my supplies on the high cache Amos and I had built, made brush beds for the dogs, cut a pile of firewood and kindling.

I was ready for the winter.

The very next day, snowshoeing across the delta of the Finlayson in search of the right kinds of logs for my cabin, I jumped and killed a moose. At my shot a second bull floundered to his feet a hundred yards away, and I downed him as well. Within two miles of my tent I had taken enough fresh meat to last the dogs and me well toward spring, provided we alternated it with fish, and I was sure that would be no problem.

I quartered the two moose, went back for the dogs, and hauled the quarters to camp, storing them on the cache.

My tent home on Frances Lake.

Then I turned the dogs loose to let them feed on the leavings. I stripped the fat from the moose and rendered it down on the stove, storing it in empty tins we had left on the cache back in the summer. I had enough to serve me through the winter as cooking fat and butter.

Next I went at the job of building my cabin. I shoveled away the snow from a level area in the lee of a high bank. I'd need forty logs fifteen feet long, as near six inches through at the top and eight at the butt as I could find, and I knew exactly where to look for them. On the delta I had located the finest stand of spruce I had seen anywhere in the country. I chose trees free of limbs for the first fifteen feet, and found I could cut and trim seven or eight a day. I hauled them to the site with the dogs and the toboggan, notched them at the ends, and began the walls of my new home.

They went up surprisingly fast. When I had a tier of four logs in place and was ready to add the next tier, I covered the first ones with a four-inch layer of moss for chinking. The tier above pressed this down to form an almost airtight joint. I built the gable ends by pegging each log to the one below it, and was ready for the roof. That would be the most difficult part of the job. I notched a stout ridge pole at both ends and laid it in place. Next I cut small poles ten feet long, laying them from the ridge down to the side walls with a generous overhang and pegging them to the top log with wooden pegs.

Thick green moss grew everywhere around the cabin. I found I could shovel away the snow and roll it up in strips like a rug. I covered the roof poles with a layer a foot thick and added a few poles to hold it in place. Finally I located unfrozen gravel at the bottom of a high bench, carried it in a bucket and spread a layer on top of the moss. When spring came I would build a better roof, but for now this one was coldproof and hopefully would not be likely to leak.

As I laid up the log walls of the cabin I had cut openings for two windows and a door. I made the door of two layers of poles with moss tamped tightly between, and hung it with wooden hinges so that it fitted snugly. I had bought a roll of isinglass from the Dease Lake post for the windows. It was not clear but it let light through, about like the side curtains on an old Model T touring car.

At last my new home was ready for occupancy and I moved in. That was a great day. There may be things in life more satisfying than building a warm cabin with your own hands hundreds of miles from the nearest source of materials or help, and knowing it will shelter you against winter cold—but I have not discovered them.

Living in the tent had been a sorry experience. The little camp stove, only eighteen by fourteen inches, was fine for cooking but would not hold heat unless it was fed with wood continually. For greater comfort I had often built an open fire a few feet in front of the tent. It heated the opening but not the interior.

At thirty below zero the cold poured through the tent roof like a stream of ice water. The walls and roof became covered with frost, glistening like diamonds in the candle-light. The inside temperature dropped to zero night after night, and my water bucket froze solidly almost to the bottom.

Leaving the misery of tent life for the warmth of the

cabin was a welcome change. For a few hours the new walls and roof sweated from melting frost, but then the place turned warm enough. I could even strip and take a bath, a luxury that had been denied me for weeks. I made a bunk and table, a bench for the stove and a shelf or two, all from small poles. The cabin assumed some degree of comfort and convenience.

Winter had clamped down in earnest now. The open water of the lake froze and snow lay deep over the land. The temperature hovered at around forty below, dropping down to fifty or sixty now and then. I piled up a big reserve of stove wood.

One morning I harnessed the dogs and set out to explore the upper end of Frances Lake, above the delta of the Finlayson. The dogs and I had traveled about a dozen miles, following a small frozen river beyond the head of the lake, when I saw a band of wild sheep licking at clay banks a short distance ahead. I had found a natural salt lick. The sheep had come down from a mountain to the west and their trails were all over the place. If I had had any doubt about a supply of fresh meat for the remainder of the winter, it was ended now. The salt-hungry sheep would use this place until spring, and of all the wild meat available in that country theirs was the most flavorful.

I shot two of them, dressed them, loaded the carcasses on the toboggan, and turned the dogs back toward the cabin. That was a jubilant homecoming, in the failing light of a cold winter afternoon.

By this time I had taken the floats off my gill net and stretched it under the ice of the lake a hundred feet from shore. I was catching all the whitefish I and the dogs could use, and now and then a lake trout. To lift the net I chopped a hole in the ice around the poles that anchored each end of it and pulled it out onto the ice, allowing a rope at the other end to pay out. When I had retrieved my catch, I pulled it back under the ice with that rope and anchored it again with the poles.

A few days after I had found the sheep lick I saw a band of caribou string out across the lake three or four miles down from the cabin. They had come down the Il-es-tooa River, following the low brush on which they feed in winter. I watched them through my powerful field glasses as they crossed the lake. There must have been three hundred of them, romping and playing in the thirty-below clear air. Some of the young ones ran out from the herd, and, kicking up the snow as they ran, skidded suddenly to a stop, quickly turning their heads to see the spray of snow they had created. Some lunged with their antlers against others, in mock battle, like children playing on the school lot back home, then backed off, only to repeat it again and again. I watched them play, sometimes one throwing another down, then prancing around in the joy of victory until the conquered would leap up and give chase across the lake ice.

Seeing them play like one big family with not a care in the world made me feel suddenly very lonely. With the knowledge that Christmas was only a few days off, the sight and silence touched some key of memory and I found myself reflecting on Christmas days full of joy and laughter I had enjoyed in my childhood, surrounded by my family. Somehow, I thought, if I could join those happy caribou, if I could touch them and talk to them, it would give me a sense of companionship.

Knowing that they would stampede from a strange scent, I made plans. Early the next morning I hitched up my dogs to the toboggan, and armed with pick and shovel, mushed up the frozen lake and river to the salt lick. I broke loose a few hundred pounds of the frozen muck and loaded it onto the toboggan. The next day I mushed down the lake to the delta of the Il-es-tooa. I broke the salty clay chunks and spread them out among the caribou brush. Knowing that my scent would be where I had touched the brush, I could only hope that the caribou would tolerate the man scent in their anxiety to lick salt.

The next day, looking through my field glasses, I saw the leader come, gingerly at first, then apparently approving. He began to lick. Almost immediately the rest of the herd followed. In threes and fives and scattered throughout, they stumbled out from the shelter of the poplar trees onto the delta, and began licking the salt, nibbling occasionally at the brush. Every once in a while one of them would raise his head with a jerk, and I could almost hear him snort as he touched brush scented by man, but he would settle back and lick his beloved salty clay.

The next day I mushed up the river again and recovered more salt from the lick. It was an all-day job, twenty-four miles round trip, but the trail was hard packed from the day before and the dogs wagged their bushy tails high over their backs all day. Before turning into bed I marked off the day with an X on the calendar. Tomorrow would be Christmas Eve. The cold weather was holding so it would likely stay clear the next few days. In the morning the dogs jumped and barked as I took the harness off its pegs on the cabin wall. We ran the few miles to the delta again, and I planted the salt as before, scattering it widely over the delta; then I went home and tied the dogs to their kennels. It was already quite dark and the stars were bright when I got back to the cabin. Tomorrow would be Christmas Day, and I would try a lonely experiment.

Before true daylight I snowshoed down the lake to the Il-es-tooa, made myself comfortable under a big poplar, and waited for the caribou.

Unless you have seen a herd of three or four hundred caribou, you have little idea of the fearlessness of the herd. They will face and kill a pack of wolves or any natural enemy. Could the desire for salt overcome the fear of man scent? This was the test. I went unarmed except for my belt knife, which is as much a part of a woodsman's clothing as his shirt. I waited, getting colder by the minute in the stillness of thirty below, for what seemed hours. Then, quite casually, there they came.

Over the brow of the upper gravel terraces I saw the leader, his magnificent spread of antlers silhouetted against the cloudless blue sky, slowly threading his way through the light growth of trees. Closely following came his herd, feeding as they came. Unhurried, nipping the tops off the brush that stuck out through the two feet of snow, and digging the snow occasionally with the shovel-like horn growth that protrudes down over their noses, they slowly came closer to me. The big bull leader must have been twenty yards from me when he jerked up his head and snorted, turning back toward the herd. I feared they would stampede, but the big bull hesitated and in a moment turned back and cautiously came closer to me. He touched the first block of frozen salt and began to lick.

I had filled my parka pockets with table salt, in case they got close enough to me. Perhaps it was wishful thinking, but there was no one to see my foolishness. I was alone with the caribou. Slowly they came, edging closer as they grazed. I stood frozen still, my hands deep in my parka pockets. My only concern was that the caribou not be afraid of me. I only wanted greatly to be friends and to understand better these carefree, happy animals.

Soon they were licking the salt blocks all around me. One, a small bull, came up close to me, and I ventured to hold out my hand full of table salt. At my arm movement he reared up and I thought for a moment that he meant to strike me down. Shaking his head he backed off a few steps and then resumed licking salty clay, eyeing me the while. Another caribou came close, between the first bull and me. He seemed less fearful, coming close so that I could almost reach him with an outstretched hand. I moved, tossing a little free salt. His head came up instantly, but he did not move his legs, and slowly he resumed licking. I had won. The desire for salt had overcome the fear of human scent and even the sight of me.

I stepped out from my tree in slow motion. Gingerly I approached the nearest caribou. To my surprise and joy he seemed undisturbed. Slowly I held out a handful of table salt. He leaned his beautiful antlered head down, sniffing from a foot away. Frozen, hardly breathing, I stood stock still, keeping my outstretched hand steady. The beautiful head leaned out, as I prayed that it would, and he licked the salt from my hand.

Have you ever had great faith in something, and had your innermost desire answered? It is a wonderful and most satisfying thing. To feel the confidence of that cold and wet nose snuffing into my hand of salt, an animal truly of the wilderness, unafraid, licking my hand—what a glorious, triumphant, happy feeling! I had a terrific sense of accomplishment, of being at one with all of nature.

That moment will live with me forever. Calmly I moved slowly into the herd. For a long time I *walked* with the herd as they grazed out to the lake's edge, licking the salt blocks everywhere. None seemed to fear me; I was accepted as one of them. Shuffling my snowshoes ahead quietly and avoiding any quick movement I was able to move among them— holding out my hand with its salt to one after another— and have them lick it clean. As I moved out onto the lake ice they followed.

Even as I left them, snowshoeing over my broken trail toward the cabin three miles away, one or two followed close, looking for more salt. Indeed, God was in His Heaven that Christmas Day.

That day was mine.

12
I ADMIRE WOLVES

So gaunt against the gibbous moon,
Piercing the silence velvet-piled,
A lone wolf howls his ancient rune—
The fell arch-spirit of the Wild.
                              —"The Land God Forgot"

I began now to make preparations for spring. I had fashioned a sawpit on four tall stumps, like the one Amos and I
had used when we built the *Come What May* at Dease
Lake. It was in a fine stand of spruce, with plenty of big
trees that would cut into twelve-foot logs, the length of
board I needed for the flume and sluice box I was planning.

I felled the trees, cut them into twelve-foot lengths with
the crosscut saw, hauled them into place with the help of
the dogs and rolled them up the sloping skids to the top of
the frame. Sometimes I found myself astonished at the
things an able-bodied and self-reliant man could do without
help.

Next I started to whipsaw the boards. I had thought
whipsawing was a devilish job when Amos and I cut the
lumber for our boat. But now, doing it alone, I found it more
than twice as hard.

I made the same blackened chalk line Amos and I had
used but found quickly that it was almost impossible to
keep the saw from wandering off that line. Time after time

I jumped down into the sawpit and tried to work from below, twisting the saw to bring it back where I wanted it. This helped, but not a great deal.

Next I tried turning the log end-for-end and cutting in the opposite direction so the two cuts would meet. But that whipsaw seemed to have a will of its own and simply wouldn't make a straight cut. I shaped long tapering wedges from a birch and drove them into the cut to open it. That also helped, but not enough. Now and then, however, the wedges would split a straight-grained log, and when that happened I had only to smooth the resulting board with my ax.

There was no hurry, for I had the rest of the winter with nothing else to do. I took my time. Luckily, for the flume and sluice box I did not need boards as smooth and true as Amos and I had fashioned.

As January wore on the pressure of work slackened, and for all my love of solitude I began to feel an urge for companionship. I had not seen another human being since I left Lower Post at the beginning of winter, and I was getting lonesome. I knew what I wanted to do: I'd go shopping.

I badly needed a bigger stove to heat the cabin. My little camp stove was entirely inadequate. It would be fun, too, to get a few food luxuries. I had learned from the Indians back in the summer that there was a trading post over the divide on the Pelly River at Pelly Banks, some seventy-five miles by rough trail northwest of my cabin. It was one of a dozen scattered on the side streams of the Yukon basin, belonging to the Taylor & Drury Company, an outfit that had its headquarters and main store in Whitehorse.

The trail led up the Finlayson River, the Indians had said, along the northeast side of Finlayson Lake, and then down a creek to the Pelly. The trip would do the dogs good and would be a break for me.

I had sold some of my summer's poke of gold in Telegraph Creek, taking in exchange a letter of credit good at any Hudson's Bay Company post, plus some ten- and twenty-dollar gold pieces. I knew that Indians understood and accepted gold coins, but had absolutely no confidence in paper money—maybe because few of them could read and so could not tell one denomination from another. But in the farthest interior, gold coins or metal trade tokens issued by the trading companies passed among them readily.

I started my trip with a light load on the toboggan, only a canvas fly and my bedroll, ax and gun, a small grub box, and meat for the dogs. Their daily ration was five pounds apiece, and they always downed it in two or three gulps as if half starved. We made thirty miles the first day and reached Finlayson Lake the day after. There two caribou broke from the cover of the timber and started across the lake when they heard us approaching. I shot both of them, built a high cache and put the eight quarters on it. The meat would be there in an emergency, and I'd pick up as much as we needed on the return trip. Caribou trails wound in every direction near the lake. Plainly this was a major wintering ground for the northern herds.

Late the third day, following a small creek down to the Pelly, we hit a well-broken toboggan trail, a trapper's line with snowshoe trails leading off to his sets. Shortly after that we heard dogs howling, and then the trail topped a rise and there were a dozen cabins strung along the bank of a good-sized river. We were at Pelly Banks Post, the most isolated of any in the upper Yukon country. As late as the 1940s, maps of that area still showed the creeks in dotted lines, indicating that their exact location and source were not known.

The trader in charge of the post was Van Gorder, a powerfully built, barrel-chested, six-foot Virginian who had come to the North many years before and stayed because he liked the country and the freedom it afforded. He had an Indian wife and a family of children, and was a completely happy man, ruling a small empire firmly, but respected and liked by the Indians. He was also a good host.

He invited me to dinner, and while we ate I learned that there were three other white men in the Pelly River area, all trappers. He put me up for the night in a well-built cabin that belonged to the police but was not in use in

The team rests on the Finlayson River trail around the canyon.

winter. It was occupied only when the Mountie made his annual summer visit to the post.

I bought a big barrel-type heating stove, a case of raisins, a drum of dried milk, and a few other supplies. Prices were high, for understandable reasons. All freight had to be brought from Seattle or Vancouver to Skagway, a distance of one thousand miles, by steamer. From Skagway it moved over the Coastal Range on the White Pass and Yukon Railroad to Whitehorse at the head of the Yukon River.

From Whitehorse it was taken down that river to Fort

Selkirk, two hundred and fifty miles, aboard the *Yukon Rose,* a small steamer belonging to the Taylor & Drury Company, and then another two hundred and fifty miles up the Pelly to Ross Post.

Because of the rapids in Hoole Canyon, above Ross Post, the trade goods had to be moved the last seventy-five miles up the Pelly to Pelly Banks by poling boat, and that final leg included a portage around the canyon.

In all, about six hundred roundabout river miles, some of them very hard miles, were involved between Whitehorse and Pelly Banks Post, plus costs on the railroad and the coastal steamers to Skagway. It was hardly a wonder that every white man here learned quickly to be a good hunter, and grew a vegetable garden at his cabin.

I loaded my supplies and mushed out at daylight the next morning. We had come as far as the head of Finlayson Lake on the way home when I witnessed the most dramatic display of the hunting methods of wolves I have ever seen.

Near the lake the country flattened out into a swampy area, frozen smooth and solid, making easy travel for the dogs. As we came to the shore I saw a lone caribou break from the timber ahead and run full tilt out onto the ice. Seconds later a huge black wolf leaped down from the low bank in close pursuit. Behind him came a tawny red wolf, slightly smaller, and five younger ones, mostly gray. I recognized the pack instantly. They were the same family group that I had watched frequently crossing Frances Lake or playing on the ice near my cabin. They were more than fifty miles from there now, which affords some idea of the ability of wolves to travel.

Their long muscular bodies flowed over the snow as if carried on the wind. The chase of the caribou must have been a long one, through heavy timber, for in open country the caribou would simply have faded away from the wolves with little effort. As it was, they gained on him with every stride.

The black leader came even with the hind legs of the caribou, turned his head and slashed at a leg without slackening pace. By that time the red bitch was shoulder to shoulder with him, and he swerved away to let her take his place. She slashed instantly, just as he had done.

The caribou stumbled and almost went down. He regained his feet, but his left hind leg dragged useless. The wolves had cut or injured the hamstring.

Now it was the turn of the pups. They came racing up on the right side and the first two slashed at their victim. The caribou went down, staggered half up and sank back on his haunches, both hind legs disabled.

The black leader was standing about twenty yards off, with the bitch beside him. Together they watched the pups circle and close in.

By that time I had freed my .30/06 Winchester from the top lashings of the toboggan. I could have killed any one of the wolves, maybe two or three before they raced beyond range. I could also have killed the caribou and spared him the agony of slow death. But I held my fire, spellbound by what I had witnessed, overcome with admiration for the teamwork and perfect discipline of that savage pack. It had been like watching a carefully rehearsed play in which each actor understood his role and performed flawlessly.

I hushed my dogs to keep them from yelping or barking, and waited.

The leader and his bitch moved in slowly, drifting closer and closer to the doomed caribou. Disabled as he was, he was still dangerous and the wolves knew it. He could no longer run but he could split the skull of any member of the pack with a single blow of a forehoof.

The two old ones took up positions ten or a dozen steps away, and the five pups gathered in a semicircle around him, waiting—patient and deadly. Then as if at a signal three of the youngsters feinted toward the head of their victim, dangerously close. The caribou reared to strike, but in that same instant the leader flashed in from one side and struck the caribou behind a shoulder with his full weight.

I suppose my sympathies should have been with the loser in that pitiless attack. For the most part man is inclined to take the side of the underdog, and the caribou had never had a chance. But I didn't feel that way. The wolves were predators—but so was, I. I had quarters of moose, sheep, and caribou on my own caches at that very minute. They were killing for the same reason I killed, because it meant food—and because they were born to it. Well, they had as much right to take a caribou as I did, I told myself.

The blow of the black wolf had knocked the bull over on his side, and the pack was on him in a flash, tearing at his throat and belly. His ordeal was quickly finished. One wolf slashed through the jugular and the caribou kicked a few times and was dead.

One of my dogs barked, and the wolves stopped feeding and pricked up their ears. I had seen enough, and besides, I wanted the caribou quarters for dog food. I sent a shot over their backs, and at the whiplash report of the rifle they scattered and raced for the cover of the timber on shore.

Back at the cabin I settled once more into my solitary winter routine. Stoked with half-green logs, my new stove burned steadily all night. For the first time since I had arrived at Frances Lake my water bucket did not freeze, and the cabin stayed snug and warm all day.

I went back to the sawpit and cut enough boards for a cabin floor as well as for the flume and sluice box. I hauled the lumber for the mine across the delta and up the frozen Finlayson River to the Half-Moon.

On one such trip I saw a family of otters at play. They had made their home in a gravel bank where a low bench sloped down into a gulley a few feet back from the river. They must have made a tunnel from their den down through the gravel into the river at a level below the ice, so that they could hunt fish. They had made a slide on the snowbank from the top of a fifteen-foot bench down to the river. As I watched they followed one another in turn, climbing the steep bank on their short legs, then trotting a few feet to the top of the slide. Then they just flopped on their bellies and glided down the steep, icy slope, swishing out onto the river ice. They were like a bunch of kids at play on a slide into a swimming pool. There were five in the family. Papa otter was huge, even for a full-grown male. He must have measured four feet long with his big flattened head and whiskers sticking out each side like a seal, the slender and sleek body ending in a heavy tapering tail. He had short legs with large webbed feet and seemed rather clumsy when running, yet he was the most graceful and the fastest swimmer imaginable. Mama otter was about a foot shorter and maybe a little more plump, but she ran up the steep slope and slid down just as fast and happily as the others. The three youngsters were noticeably smaller, not over two feet long. The young ones tried to pass each other while climbing up the hill, which resulted in collisions and often two of them sliding down together.

From then on I observed them often. They would sometimes play on that slide for hours on end, then disappear into their den or swim under the ice and into the huge lake. There was limitless food for them in the lake, and I feared only that one might get caught in my gill net.

I decided to build a boat for summer fun and for hunting and fishing, so single-handed I cut what lumber I'd need for a fourteen-foot lake boat.

In March, when the lengthening days began to signal the end of winter, the Indians came back from their trapping grounds. They arrived one day at sunset with their families loaded on the toboggans, the dog teams strung out across the lake, an age-old cavalcade of the North country.

They made their camp on the little creek below my cabin, retrieving the tent poles they had stacked against trees the previous fall. Some had tents, others set the poles in circles and covered them with pieces of old canvas and skins to make tepees. They staked out their dogs, built fires, and hung kettles of meat to cook. Then Caesar and Little Jimmy came to visit me.

Had they found me with a trapline, I'm sure they would have shown strong resentment; I might even have been in danger. But when they saw that I was holed up in my cabin, with a packed trail leading up the Finlayson toward my gold claim, and they saw my pile of whipsawed lumber, they knew I had come to mine and they were all smiles.

To Caesar I said, "I dig for gold this summer. You come work for me? Maybe two, three men work. I pay trade goods or gold dollars."

A smile crossed his face at the mention of gold dollars. He said: "Finish beaver hunt, we come work."

13
SUMMER AT THE HALF-MOON

I've sweated athirst in its summer heat, I've frozen and
starved in its cold;
I've followed my dreams by its thousand streams, I've
toiled and moiled for its gold.
—"The Parson's Son"

That spring of 1926 took its own time arriving, after the fashion of springs in the Yukon. Maybe it seemed slower than usual to me because of my impatience to begin work at the Half-Moon.

The snow on the lake melted and pools of water covered the ice, freezing at night, thawing by midday. The ice began its March booming, deep rolling thunder echoing across it as it cracked and lifted with the rising water beneath it, an unfailing harbinger of the coming breakup. The Indians left again, to go on their annual spring beaver hunt, and I was by myself once more. They would not return before early June.

I pitched my tent at the Half-Moon now, and began work on sluice boxes and flume. A flock of swans landed on the ice of Frances Lake one afternoon, the first I had seen in the North. Flocks of geese passed over frequently, and I finally climbed the benches along the Finlayson to the small lakes where I had seen them slant down to land, and collected the makings of a goose dinner. The oven of my little stove was too small to accommodate such a bird, but I cleaned the goose, left the feathers on, coated it with clay and baked it in the hot coals of my fire from morning of one day until noon of the next. The clay, feathers, and skin came away together in big pieces, and I had never eaten a more tasty fowl.

The freezing nights prevented me from starting my gold operation, so I put in my time building the boat I wanted. I finished it with two pairs of oars and a mast mounted through the forward seat. My canvas toboggan cover would serve as a makeshift sail. By the time that job was finished, the gravel at the Half-Moon was thawed sufficiently that I could break it up with a shovel. I rigged my flume, a long, sloping chute to bring water down where I wanted it, and at the end of it a sluice box twenty-four feet long where the actual washing of the gravel would be done.

Spring began to hurry along now. Wide cracks opened across the lake, and then the wind changed direction and there were a hundred yards of open water along the beach in front of my cabin. I widened the trail from the cabin to the mine and freed it of windfalls. I intended to continue living at the cabin, hiking back and forth each morning and evening. It was far more comfortable there than in the tent and the mosquitoes would not be as bad on the lake shore as in the brushy canyon. Besides, there were things I wanted to do around the cabin. I'd even plant a small garden, with seeds I had brought in back in the fall.

It was exciting to see the water flowing freely through the long line of boxes and to throw in the first shovels of pay dirt. I shoveled and washed gravel for ten days before I shut water out of the sluice box and made my first cleanup. In that ten days I had washed $180 worth of gold, which would be nine ounces, or about $6 a yard!

The ice went completely out of the lake and ducks started to nest along the shore. I searched out a few of the nests and added eggs to my diet of meat and fish and bannock. The test for freshness was simple. I laid an egg in the palm of my hand and held it under water. If the egg stayed submerged it was all right to eat. If it floated up it was growing a little duck inside.

Early in June Caesar and Little Jimmy, Chief Smith and Oaltal, Meegan and the Old Chief all returned with their families to their summer camp. The spring beaver hunt was finished. A few days later two of the men took off with pack dogs, headed for Lower Post with the winter's catch of furs. In exchange, they would bring back tea and salt, ammunition and more traps. If the fur catch fetched enough in trade, they'd also bring a few luxuries, cotton print dresses and bright head scarves for the women and overalls and shirts for the men. Finally, if their credit permitted, some rice and sugar.

Caesar and his wide-grinning wife came to the cabin one evening and I shared my tobacco with them. While we smoked we reached an agreement for him and Little Jimmy to go to work for me at the mine.

Neither of the Indians had ever used a pick or shovel, and they were awkward at first. But they soon got the hang of it, and were able to keep the tailings clear at the lower end of the sluice box as fast as I shoveled gravel in at the head. Jimmy also cleared away the light brush and small trees over an area where we planned to mine as the summer went along.

High water interrupted us. With the melting snow the Finlayson began to roar down its canyon and rocks half as big as a bushel basket came tumbling and grinding along with the current. We loaded boulders on top of the flume intake to hold it in place, and went on with our mining as soon as we could. Gold mining, I was learning, meant twelve to sixteen hours a day of hard labor.

The long days of summer came and crested. Wild fruit ripened everywhere and I feasted on currants and raspberries and then, in August, on blueberries. Grouse were plentiful and fat, and as often as we needed it I shot a moose. The Indians welcomed the fresh meat, and there were enough families in camp that none of it was ever wasted.

My little garden began to pay off. Radishes, lettuce, and carrots grew in profusion, turnips and other vegetables did reasonably well. Rabbits found the young lettuce and threatened to harvest the entire crop, until I chained one of my dogs close by the vegetable patch.

I was living a king's life, working hard but enjoying it, hard and muscular as a man could get. In the three years I had been in the North I had suffered no real illness. I had been snow-blind once, my own fault, and had frozen my fingers and toes a few times, but never severely enough to leave lasting damage. Apart from those minor mishaps I had not had an ache or pain, not even a toothache.

I was fully accepted by the Indians now as a member of their community. Whenever I got into my boat for a sail across the lake, half a dozen youngsters splashed out to join me. They learned to row with the big clumsy oars I had made, laughing and singing their curious lilting songs. The girls were better at rowing than the boys, and often I would find a group of them waiting by the boat where it was pulled up on the beach, hoping I would take them out on the water.

One evening we had a big barbecue on the beach, attended by everybody in camp. I had shot a moose. The women took the whole sides of rib, built a long fire and stood the two rib racks up on end on clean spruce boughs, one on either side of the fire, propped upright with sticks.

They had started the cooking in late afternoon. The meat roasted slowly, browning and dripping fat. When we came down the trail from the mine that evening all the families were waiting for us, and the barbecue was ready.

The men served themselves first, each one cutting away a big rib. Next the women sliced off chunks for the children, and finally for themselves. Eventually everybody was squatting on his haunches with a big piece of meat and a hunting knife, wolfing the food down as if it were his first real meal in a month. I ate as ravenously as the Indians. It would be hard to find more tasty meat than fresh, fat moose ribs, barbecued in that fashion over an open fire. There was much merriment and singing around the fire that night, little of which I could understand, but it was a night to remember.

I had at least two of the Indians working with me at the mine every day now, sometimes three for a few days at a time. They had become accustomed to using a shovel, and two of us could shovel gravel into the sluice box from opposite sides, while a third man kept the tailings cleared away. Every ten days I cleaned up the box and added the take of gold to the pokes that lay stacked along the edge of my table. For three weeks at a stretch we had lean washing. Then we hit a rich pay streak again, and the pokes grew. I was averaging eight to ten ounces of gold a week and I felt like a millionaire.

Fortunately the Indians showed no interest in nuggets or dust, but they took great delight in the twenty-dollar gold pieces with which I paid them for their work.

The summer days began to shorten, and at the first hint of autumn I was aware of a growing unrest. I had been away from my own people for almost a year now and, friendly as my Indian neighbors had been, I was suddenly lonely to see white faces again, to see bright lights, listen to dance music, eat fancy food, do the things that white men do even in the far-off outposts of civilization. The urge to go Outside was mounting in me and I realized the time had come. I did not want to spend another winter in solitude here at Frances Lake, at least not now. I needed a holiday.

I laid my plans carefully. I'd keep on working at the Half-Moon until mid-September, as Amos and I had done the year before. I'd have everything in readiness to leave, and when the day came I would need only to shut the cabin door and go. My possessions would be safe on the high cache until I came back, whenever that might be.

I'd take the dogs in the boat to the foot of the lake, where the Indian trail to Lower Post began, the trail I had followed when I came to Frances Lake back in the winter. I'd beach the boat there, pack the dogs, and hike out to Lower Post. Somebody would take me across the Liard, and I could then follow the trail along the Dease up to Dease Lake. It would take many days, but it was the quickest and safest way out for a man by himself.

I'd leave the dogs in Telegraph Creek to be boarded again, or take them down to Wrangell and leave them there. I was going on to Vancouver this time. I wanted to see a city again. If all went well, I'd be there about the middle of October. I'd sell my gold at the Government Assay Office in Vancouver, and that way I could keep my discovery concealed.

The clear days of fall came quickly, with heavy frosts at night. Ice began to rim the sluice boxes and form along the edges of the flume. It was time to shut down. With the help of my Indian crew I pulled the flume apart and stacked it and the boxes at the foot of a steep slope, safely out of reach of the river. I had netted and smoked two hundred whitefish for the trip, and another five hundred were stored on the cache to serve as a safe supply of dog food when I returned. The Indians and I had a last feast on the beach, and at dark the next evening I was at the foot of Frances Lake with the dogs. I pulled the boat up and turned it over, and at first light the following morning we took the long trail that would end at Telegraph Creek.

It was a trip without incident, except that one of the dogs held us up for a half day when he tangled with a porcupine and came running to me, his snout bristling with quills. He looked comical with his whole nose white with quills, but I knew he must be in great pain. There is an art to removing quills; they can tear the flesh badly. A porky quill has a barb on the end that makes it painful to pull out, but the quill is hollow and filled with air, like a tube tapered and sealed at both ends. By cutting off the end of the quill you can flatten it, thus relieving the pressure from the point. If vinegar is then allowed to run onto the wounds it softens the quill points so that they may be pulled out almost painlessly. I pulled out the mess of quills from Runt's nose and reminded him that every dog has to learn to leave porcupines alone.

The trail seemed shorter than the long four hundred miles over which I had driven the dogs the previous November; perhaps trails always seem shorter the second time over. We arrived at Telegraph Creek and I spent an evening with my friend Harry Dodd, the Gold Commissioner. He was the only person to whom I confided the story of Half-Moon, along with something of my future plans. I had no inkling how quickly those plans would be changed.

I made the trip downriver to Wrangell on the *Hazel B No. 2*, the boat that had brought me to Telegraph Creek almost three and a half years before. Even I found it hard to believe the changes that had occurred in me in those forty months.

I had wanted to eat beef again. Now, after a diet of moose and caribou, I found beef flat and tasteless. I had wanted to hear English speech and dance music. But the voices sounded too loud and the jazz music in the cafés grated on my wilderness-attuned ears. There seemed to be nowhere I could go to get away from the noise. I also discovered that my sense of smell had become highly refined and selective. I could scent a horse a block away, or chickens that were out of sight in a backyard behind a store.

But there were some things about civilization that I delighted in as much as I had expected to. Fresh butter and oranges, tomatoes and cake, for example, and the luxury of a hot bath in a tub.

One thing really surprised me. My own speech had degenerated into broken English from long contact with the Indians. My undiluted mother tongue came back with difficulty.

To inquisitive strangers who spotted me as a prospector fresh out of the bush, and inquired what luck I had had, I showed samples of the high-grade galena ore that lay waiting on the east arm of Frances Lake. I was not yet ready to share with anyone the story of my gold discovery. My questioners looked at the galena, measured mentally the wilderness miles to the place where we had taken the samples, grinned, and shook their heads. My secret stayed safe.

I loafed for two days in Wrangell, waiting for the steamer to Vancouver. I left my dogs, boarded the *Princess Louise* when she docked the second evening, and enjoyed a leisurely three-day cruise south through the Inside Passage.

On a clear October day we tied up at the Vancouver dock, the same dock from which Anton Money, the green cheechako fresh out from England, had left for his beloved North three and a half years earlier.

14
JOYCE

There comes the mad-blood clamour for a woman's
  clinging hand,
Love-humid eyes, the velvet of a breast.
  —"The Squaw Man"

My first errand in Vancouver was at the Government Assay
Office.

I learned there that they could tell from an assay from
what creek a poke of gold came, since that from each location varied in purity. In the case of mine, it was from a new
and unrecorded discovery and I was told that I would have
to declare where I had gotten it. I was very reluctant, lest
my secret leak out, but I was assured there was no cause
for worry. The officials were sworn to silence, unless they
had reason to suspect the gold was stolen, in which case
they turned the investigation over to the police.

They were greatly interested in my find and even re-
spectful of it, and I was treated with the utmost courtesy.
At the end I was told to come back in three days for my
check.

My summer of washing gold at Half-Moon had netted
me $2,280. I had recovered approximately an ounce a day,
from early May until I left in September.

That same sum of money would have eight to ten times
the purchasing power today it had at that time, when a

laborer was lucky to make $4.50 a day. For a man of twenty-six, who had come out from England three years before at $125 a month, that $2,280 was a small fortune. My hard work and lonely way of life at Frances Lake had paid handsomely.

The next thing I did was buy some new clothes. Those I had come out with, stored in Telegraph Creek for more than three years, were so tight that I was embarrassed to wear them. Not that they had shrunk. Their wearer had developed new muscles over all his body, muscles they could not accommodate.

Even in clothing that fitted, I still attracted attention and people stared at me on the street. I was tanned darker than most Indians, but at the same time my blond hair had been bleached white by the sun, and the contrast was startling.

I moved into a quiet hotel where the meals were excellent and where I had a fine room overlooking ocean and mountains. For a time traffic noise bothered me and I awoke every time a car went by at night. I even fell into the habit of getting up at first light and exploring the city on foot, while there were very few people on the streets.

I had had friends in Vancouver before going north. I got in touch with them, and made new ones. Invitations came thick and fast, to parties and dances and beach picnics, and I tried to catch up on all the movies and concerts I had missed. My holiday was turning out exactly as I had wanted it to.

Among the friends I had known earlier was Sergeant Jim Cunningham of the British Columbia Provincial Police. At that time the Provincial Police were in charge of game affairs for the province. I looked Jim up and started making trips with him on the motor vessel he used as a patrol boat, taking frequent runs up the coast to check game preserves and licenses.

He and a partner and I came in from one of those trips one evening and I invited the two officers to dinner at my hotel. We were in rough outdoor clothes, wool shirts and boots, and we caused quite a stir. It was the practice of the guests at that hotel to dress for dinner. People stared at us, but after the first few minutes I paid little attention to them. I was doing some staring on my own.

Seated by herself at a corner table was a guest I had not seen in the dining room before. She was a girl apparently in her late teens, with a young and slender body and dark auburn hair that fell in waves to her waist. I thought her the most attractive person I had ever laid eyes on.

After my long and lonely months in the mountains I was hungry for the friendship and companionship of a pretty girl. And I suppose I was lonely for the love of a pretty girl as well, for at twenty-six Englishmen are no more phlegmatic in that regard than other men. And this girl was very pretty. I remarked about her to my two companions, but drew only the kidding retort that I had been in the woods so long I was vulnerable. That did nothing to change my mind.

After dinner I saw her again, sitting with a group of elderly women in front of the fire in the hotel lobby. One of the group was a dignified old lady whom I had met earlier. She was beside the pretty redhead and when I walked up to her she had no choice but to introduce me.

I found myself looking into a pair of clear hazel eyes that looked levelly back at me, and suddenly I was aware that my heart was pounding. I had dated a great many girls; in England after the war I had averaged a new one every week or two. But nothing like this had ever happened to me.

Her name was Joyce Curtis, and she was seventeen. Her father was a doctor back in Rochester, New York, and she was in Vancouver by herself, ready to begin training as a nurse.

I think we both knew in the first instant our eyes met and locked that we were meant for each other.

We sat and talked long after the older women had left to go to their rooms and the fire had died. She was fascinated by the stories I told her of the North country I loved, of my months of solitude at Frances Lake, of my Indian neighbors and the ways of caribou and wolves and sled dogs.

I had met her on a Friday evening. We met again for breakfast the next morning by agreement, and spent most of that Saturday walking in Stanley Park, a beautiful and secluded place of huge fir trees with shafts of sunlight slanting down to the moss-covered trails, and glimpses of the ocean on three sides. I had always been one to make quick decisions, and by now my mind was made up. The moment we found ourselves in a place of privacy under a towering fir, I held out my arms to her.

She knew what was coming and showed no hesitancy. She came to me, I felt soft warm arms around my neck, and our lips met and clung in a long and ardent kiss.

When we broke apart I said quickly, "When will you marry me, Joyce?"

She pulled me to her again and answered in a half-teasing voice, "Will Monday be soon enough?"

Our engagement lasted through the rest of Saturday and Sunday. I knew a minister in Vancouver, the Reverend C. C. Owens, chaplain for Canadian forces from that city in World War I. I had met him through a veterans' organization. When I went to him on Monday morning and told him what I wanted, he said at first it would be impossible. But I refused to take no for an answer, and in the end he yielded to my determination. He got his church heated up, I collected half a dozen friends, and Joyce's sister and brother-in-law hurried north from Seattle. At eight o'clock that Monday evening the lovely seventeen-year-old I had met three days earlier was my wife. The date was November 10, 1926.

I awoke in the half light of dawn the next morning and lay for a time looking at her. I told myself I was the luckiest man alive.

We rented a house in West Vancouver and started to make plans to go back to Half-Moon in the early spring. We learned that we could ship supplies and equipment from Whitehorse to Pelly Banks by way of the Yukon and Pelly rivers. The Taylor & Drury Company would handle the details. From the Pelly Banks Post I could freight our outfit by dog team over the snow to Frances Lake, using the trail I had followed the previous winter. That meant we would have to be there before the snow went off, but that was no problem.

I warned Joyce of the cold and the hardships, the primitive way of life, the complete isolation, especially in winter when we would not even have Indian families near us. But she had fallen as much in love with the North as I had, without even seeing it. Everything about it intrigued her— my descriptions of its beauty and silences, of the lakes and rivers and mountains, my stories of hunting and fishing and traveling, of the excitement of finding gold. She reveled in the moccasins, the snowshoes, the skin clothing I showed her.

As for being by ourselves, the two of us alone in that limitless wilderness, nothing could have suited her better. We were terribly in love and as long as we had each other we would not miss other companionship.

Joyce was as eager to be away as I was, and we fixed the beginning of March as the time of our departure.

I went to wholesale houses in Vancouver and sent two tons of supplies and household goods north to Whitehorse. At that point a minor hitch developed. They could not reach Pelly Banks before midsummer. But we could manage. We would take the lighter items over the Finlayson River trail by pack dog, and when the first snow came in the fall we'd move the heavy stuff by toboggan.

In early March we headed north.

Joyce had never been on a big steamer before, and the cruise up the Inside Passage to Wrangell was pure delight for both of us. Snow still glistened white on the mountains of the Coast Range, but we had bought warm, windproof parkas and did not mind the weather. At that season the boat was half empty, but our fellow passengers were an interesting lot—Alaskans returning home or fur buyers on their way to northern towns for the winter catches of pelts. It was all new and fascinating to my young wife and she took to the frontier as happily as I had done four springs before.

But before we reached Wrangell something more than

a minor hitch developed. Joyce announced that she thought she was pregnant.

We were warmly welcomed in Wrangell. By that time I was regarded as an old-timer there, and the Alaskan friendships of that day were warm ones. Even my dogs were delighted to see me. But to our dismay we learned that the only doctor in town had recently left and moved south. The nearest physician now was in Juneau, another half day north by steamer.

A doctor there quickly confirmed Joyce's suspicions, and we gave up all thought of going to Frances Lake that spring. We'd stay on in Juneau, where the doctor, who treated Joyce as if she were his own daughter, could look after her and where she could have the best of care in St. Anne's Hospital when the time came for the baby to arrive.

On the way south the previous fall, I had renewed acquaintance with a trapper I had met twice before. He needed dogs on his trapline up the Iskoot River. He was reliable and good with dogs, and I agreed to let him have the use of my team in return for their keep until I needed them, which probably would not be for close to a year. The dogs would be well taken care of, fed, and exercised properly, and the arrangement was a good one for both of us.

Joyce became more and more limited in her activities, and like all young husbands I worried and fretted. But apart from our natural concerns, the summer in Juneau slipped by pleasantly enough.

Our son Sydney was born without complications in the early fall, not quite a year after our marriage. He was a healthy, happy baby, and Joyce accepted her new role as a mother as easily as she had accepted wifehood. We were so proud and elated at becoming parents that as soon as she was strong enough we took off on a two weeks' vacation, going by boat to Skagway, then over the White Pass and Yukon Railroad to Whitehorse at the head of navigation on the Yukon River.

To our surprise, a number of people there had heard of us and greeted us as old friends. They knew of me as the man from Frances Lake where, the story had it, I was developing a silver-lead showing. The consensus seemed to be that I was a bit demented to spend my time on a galena property so far from any possible transportation. But the North country residents were entirely tolerant of eccentricity, and no one put me down because of what I was doing. If I wanted to waste my time fooling around with that far-off galena deposit, it was strictly my own business. And that theory of my activities suited me perfectly. So long as no one suspected there was gold at Frances Lake, no one would start a stampede in that direction.

We took a room at the Whitehorse Inn and spent a pleasant week. The big river steamers, old-fashioned stern paddle-wheelers that plied the Yukon between Whitehorse and Dawson City four hundred and fifty miles downstream —down north—were being pulled out on the bank. Some of the tributary streams were already carrying ice and the river season was at an end for the year.

The last boat up from Dawson City brought many miners going out for the winter, by way of the narrow-gauge train on the railroad, and for a night or two Whitehorse turned into one big party. There were no locks on the doors at the hotel or on the riverboats, and unexpected company was likely to drop in at any hour of the day or night. But crime was almost unknown, and had been since the Northwest Mounted Police established law and order in the Yukon at the time of the Klondike gold rush thirty years before.

Before we left Whitehorse I checked with Taylor & Drury. My whole shipment was waiting for me now at Pelly Banks, they told me, in charge of my friend Van Gorder. All we had to do was get there before the snow went off in the spring, so we could freight the loads down the Finlayson trail to our home on Frances Lake.

Back at Juneau I returned to the job I had taken while we waited for Syd to arrive, at the Alaska-Juneau gold mine, an ore-milling operation.

We didn't really enjoy the winter in Juneau. Cold wet winds blew up the Gastineau Channel from the Taku ice fields, making the weather miserable much of the time. I wrote the trapper in Wrangell to tell him that I would need my dogs in Juneau by the first of March. We were eager to get away.

The dogs arrived on time, by steamer. We celebrated at a farewell party with our Juneau friends and headed north to Skagway and Whitehorse. There for a week we outfitted our new toboggan with a carefully selected load and drove the dogs out on test runs a few miles from town, checking the warmth and comfort of our down-filled arctic sleeping bags and our cold-weather clothing, taking special care to make sure that our wee son, not quite six months old, would not suffer from the cold on the long dogsled trip that lay ahead.

When we had made our plans to go north shortly after our wedding, we had bought heavy clothing in expectation of a late-winter journey. During the year of delay that Syd had caused we had had little use for that clothing. But now it was exactly what we would need. Joyce and I each had long one-piece underwear of pure wool, and two or three layers of heavy wool socks. In the temperatures we faced, wool next to the skin was essential. It would absorb perspiration and if we cooled off it would dry quickly. Cotton or any other nonabsorbent material would be dangerous in extremely low temperatures, meaning a severe chill or actual freezing. Over the wool underwear we wore wool shirts and heavy wool sweaters. Woolen breeches were tucked snugly into the tops of our socks.

We had been fortunate in finding two excellent parkas at a surplus store, the type used by the U.S. Expeditionary Force sent to Russia in 1919, at the close of World War I. Made of light but windproof drill, they hung loosely to below the knees. They had big slash pockets, and the cuffs were trimmed with wolverine fur, the hood was fur lined, and a heavy roll of wolverine fur made a facing around it, closing in front of the face with a drawstring. Wolverine fur was the one material that would stay free of ice in the bitterest cold. The moisture of human breath freezes quickly on any other fur, coating the face in ice, but the fur of the

Joyce in her new parka, 1929.

big weasel stays dry and protects the face from freezing, even in the teeth of a high wind.

Under the parka hoods we wore wool toques, and on our feet Indian-made moccasins. For added warmth, we folded an oblong piece of Hudson's Bay Company duffle cloth, thick wool of blanket weight, over our socks and slid the moccasins on over it. We had about an inch of wool all around our feet, insulating them from the cold, yet we could wiggle our toes freely.

That was important. It is safer to run barefoot on dry snow at thirty below than to wear a tight shoe.

The baby had his own wool outfit. He wore a thin wool shirt and socks, and a knitted bunny suit covered him completely, including feet and head, with an opening only for his face. He wore tiny moccasins made by an Indian woman in Whitehorse, and he was wrapped in a wool blanket.

Moose-skin mittens with an under mitten of blanket-weight wool completed our outfits. The mittens were hung around our necks by a bright-colored cord, to prevent dropping or losing them. At forty below, or in times of storm and bitter wind, it would not do to be bare handed while we fumbled for a dropped mitten.

We studied maps and reports of the route we were taking, and talked with local trappers and prospectors. Klondike Airways was not yet in existence as an airline at that time, but did run a tractor train from Whitehorse to Dawson City, about four hundred and fifty miles. That meant a wide, well-broken trail. The first two hundred miles of it would follow the Nordenskiold River to where that stream joined the Yukon at Carmacks.

From there we would go down the Yukon as far as Fort Selkirk where the Pelly came in, turn up that river and follow it to Pelly Banks, and then on to the Finlayson and so to Frances Lake. In all we had between six hundred and seven hundred miles of dogsled travel ahead of us, the latter half of it through wild and remote country, almost unpeopled.

We would not need to carry a heavy load of food, since we had supplies for a year waiting at Pelly Banks, seventy-five miles from the home cabin. We'd take only the mini-mum requirements for the trip itself, flour, rolled oats, rice, beans, dry milk, tea, sugar, butter and syrup, baking powder, salt and pepper. We added to that list of essentials a limited amount of dry soup mix, dried apples and peaches, raisins and dehydrated vegetables, a new experiment then. And of course dry formula for the baby.

We'd carry a slab of bacon, but for meat we would rely on ptarmigan and rabbits, which were plentiful. We could carry them frozen on the toboggan against the possibility of not finding a supply at our night camp site.

For dog feed I bought a sack of smoked and dried salmon at the Taylor & Drury store in Whitehorse. Trotting behind the dogs, I often chewed on a piece. It was no wonder the dogs liked it.

At last our arrangements were complete and we were ready for the long trail.

15

THE INCREDIBLE JOURNEY

Would she but wed me? Yes: then fared we forth
Into the vast, unvintageable North.

—*"Sunshine"*

We drove out of Whitehorse, on the tractor road that led down north toward Dawson City, at daybreak on a sparkling clear March morning when the temperature stood at twenty-five below. The town and all evidence of civilization dropped quickly out of sight.

It was the kind of weather the dogs loved. They had barked and yelped when I harnessed them, and they ran eagerly for the first half hour, then slowed to a steady, mile-eating trot. I was able to jog along behind, without snow-shoes on the hard-packed trail, hanging on to the handles of the sled. I had folded one of our sleeping bags to make a pad for Joyce on top of the load. She rode there, with her legs protected in the second bag, and held Syd on her lap. The going was easy, except that the trail was rough in spots from the tractor treads, and in those places Joyce was having a bouncing ride.

One thing we learned quickly. Extreme cold affects the kidneys of a baby more than it does those of a grownup.

Our little son wet himself about twice as frequently as normal.

His meals on the trail posed no problems. We carried cans of dry baby formula, and Joyce mixed it in the tent at night, adding dry milk and filling thermos bottles with it. Young Syd took his bottle readily, suckling and gurgling as happily as he had in the shelter of a warm room. Changing him was another matter. We had to keep him as dry as possible for safety's sake as well as for his comfort, and we knew that at twenty-five to forty-five below zero the cold could be like a branding iron on the wet skin of an infant. Each change meant stopping and building up a big open fire. It slowed our travel, but in the warmth of the fire Joyce could take care of the baby's needs in complete safety.

We stopped every two or three hours, making a pot of tea, resting the dogs, eating our own lunch if it was around noon, looking after Syd. My little family was warm and content, the trail and the weather were made to order, and Joyce and I agreed that the trip was going to be fun, as I had promised her it would.

In late afternoon we came down a long hill to the Little River Roadhouse. It was open, and although we were equipped to camp out the temptation of comfort on our first night on the trail was too much for us. We yielded, and spent the night in luxury. It would be quite a few nights before that would happen again.

We were away again at daylight. By now I realized that Joyce needed to break the tedium of sitting on the toboggan now and then, with a mile or so of walking or trotting behind it to warm her feet. I showed her how to hang onto the handlebars and jog at the pace of the six dogs, and while we laughed a lot at her stumbling on the rough trail it rested and warmed her.

The second afternoon found us at the old Nordenskiold Roadhouse. It was closed, so we made a tent camp in front of it. Some ptarmigan were flitting around the small clearing where the old buildings stood, and I shot two of them with my .22 for our supper. They were the first Joyce had ever tasted, and she thought them excellent. They are a dark-meated bird, with a flavor much like that of the grouse of Scotland.

The trail stayed brick-hard under the toboggan, but the third day the temperature started to drop, so that the little breeze created by traveling at about six miles an hour spelled danger. Late that afternoon we came to the Braeburn Roadhouse, and bunked there for the night. The wind blew hard that night and in the morning the temperature had dropped to thirty-five below. Luckily, the wind had died. Thirty-five below with a wind blowing can be far more dangerous than sixty below in still air. But even without a wind, we'd need to be very careful, watching every inch of exposed skin for frostbite, especially in the case of our little son. How do you tell when a baby feels the cold? I knew a lot about extremes of weather but very little about babies, I reflected. As often as we changed Syd that day, I built up a big pile of blazing dry logs.

Late that afternoon we came to a tree that had fallen across the trail. I shouted to the dogs to gee into the timber around it. The leader Rogue, and Rascal and Runt, the two dogs behind him, made the detour without mishap. But as the team pulled back onto the trail the fourth dog, Scotch, caught his harness on a snag.

The extreme cold must have crystallized the metal ring that held Scotch's trace, and when he lunged ahead to free himself the ring snapped in half. It was a key piece of the harness and had to be securely replaced.

I opened my emergency box of harness parts that ran across the toboggan at the tail end, found a spare ring and a length of rawhide, and started to make the repair. It was getting dusk and I was anxious to get farther along the trail and find a good camping spot. My mind was only half on what I was doing, and I did something I knew better than to do. I dropped my guard.

I had to take off my mittens to tie the rawhide. That metal ring had thirty-five below zero in it, and without thinking I grabbed it with my warm fingers and thumb. The skin and flesh stuck as if welded to the metal, and I was in trouble.

Joyce had tucked the baby down into the bedroll, climbed off the toboggan, and was stamping her feet to keep warm. I called to her to get the matches out of our grub box. Luckily, she was wearing wool gloves inside her moose-skin mittens instead of the heavier linings. She could handle the matches without taking the gloves off.

She struck one match after another, and held the tiny flames against the ring on the side away from my fingers. Slowly the metal warmed enough to release my hand. But my first and second fingers were covered with the white blisters of frostbite, and the whole face of my thumb peeled off on the ring.

The pain of thawing hard-frozen flesh has to be experienced to be believed, and I cussed myself roundly for a greenhorn, letting myself touch below-zero metal with my bare hands. I had been guilty of an instant of carelessness, and as always in the North I had paid the penalty.

Darkness was coming fast, so I decided to make camp where we were. It took longer than usual to pitch the tent and cut wood, with three very sore digits on my ax hand.

Two days later, we came out of the timber in mid-afternoon and the trail ahead led down a long slope to the pretty little settlement of Carmacks, in a triangle of land where the Nordenskiold emptied into the Yukon. Some fifty cabins and tents were strung out between the two rivers, blue wood smoke curling up from their fires, rising straight in the cold and windless air. It was a pretty sight and a welcome one.

We could see the roadhouse at the north end of town, close by the bridge that crossed the Nordenskiold, but we turned toward the Yukon bank trail instead, heading for the Taylor & Drury trading post and passing log cabins and howling dogs on the way.

Dan Snure, the trader, insisted we stay in his bungalow, since he used rooms over the store during the winter. It was cold in the unused house and it took hours for a blazing log fire in the heating stove to warm the walls and beds. But the place was comfortable then, and being in a house gave us an opportunity to wash our clothes and clean up before we tackled the next leg of our journey.

The weather turned worse during the night, and by morning it had dropped to forty-five below. We elected to stay over a day or two, for the extreme cold to break, and the people of the tiny settlement accepted us as old friends, coming to call, eager to see new faces. This was the open friendship typical of the North, I told Joyce.

Dan Snure told us of a shortcut to the Pelly River. Instead of going down the Yukon to Fort Selkirk, as we had planned, we could go up the Yukon from Carmacks to the Little Salmon, follow up that stream, cross over some high country and come down to the upper Pelly at Rose Creek. It would cut off two sides of a big triangle and save many miles of travel.

The wind finally died and the thermometer climbed to twenty below zero. We loaded up and mushed out onto the ice of the Yukon, turning upriver. The tractor trail was behind us now. A good dog trail had been broken on the river but the wind of the last two days had drifted it completely over. Still the dogs could scent it under the drifts, and it made better footing than the unbroken snow on either side.

We made the usual stops and built big open fires, and the first stars were pricking out in the clear winter sky when we pulled into the trading post at Little Salmon. We had met the trader and his wife, a couple by the name of Morrison, in Whitehorse the previous fall, and we were warmly welcomed.

The Little Salmon turned out to be a small, winding stream, protected from winds by heavy timber along its banks. The woods were laced with trappers' snowshoe trails but we saw no one, and the winter silence was complete, broken only by the crunch and creak of my snowshoes and of the hickory boards of the toboggan sliding over the dry snow, a sound like that of running your fingers through wet hair. This was winter travel at its best, through country of

Joyce riding the load with her feet in an eiderdown sleeping bag.

great beauty, and Joyce and I found ourselves singing to the dogs as we went.

I had learned by now that having a family along meant a great deal more work for me on the trail. Traveling by myself, I had rarely bothered to pitch a tent unless the weather was bad, sleeping instead in my bag on top of the toboggan, or at most under a fly in front of my campfire. Now I had to start the evening chores by building a big open fire to keep Joyce and Syd warm, and cutting a pile of green boughs for them to sit on. Next came putting up the little silk tent, flooring it with spruce boughs a foot thick, installing the small camp stove and cutting firewood. Joyce would keep herself and the boy snug by the open fire until the tent was ready and she could start cooking supper. I tied the dogs to separate trees, out of reach of one another, fed them their ration of smoked salmon, ran the toboggan up with a log under each end to keep it from freezing down to the snow, and lashed the load securely in case a dog got loose during the night. For water, once in a while we could find an open patch free of ice, but most of the time we had to melt snow. A large pail of the dry and powdery snow of the North yields surprisingly little water.

To make seven or eight hours of travel a day meant getting up at four or five o'clock in the morning and breaking camp in the dark, as soon as the family had dressed and eaten. While they kept warm by the open fire again, I loaded the sled, keeping the lunch box and tea pail where they were easily accessible. Last of all I hitched the dogs. We mushed out by daylight, and at the end of each day I was about as exhausted as a man can be. But having my wife and son with me made it more than worthwhile.

Our meals were no problem, except that it was hard to mix proper food for a six-month-old child on the trail in such weather, and we worried about Syd. But we managed all right with two large thermos bottles during the day and special foods cooked in the tent at night, and he was getting along very well, bothered by nothing as long as we made frequent stops, built up a fire and kept him dry.

For supper we usually fried a grouse or rabbit and boiled rice. We tried the new dehydrated spinach and carrots, and they were edible but far from tasty. The dried fruit was good, and Joyce strained it for the baby's supper. For breakfast we made hotcakes and bacon, served with maple syrup, or rolled oats with dry milk and sugar. Once we reached the higher country at the headwaters of the Little Salmon, I planned to shoot a caribou and augment our meat supply.

The river narrowed as we climbed toward the mountains, with here and there a wider flat. These would be swamps in summer. Now they were snow covered and smooth.

Approaching one such place, we saw mist rising off the ice like the smoke from a dozen campfires. I knew what that meant. The ice had cracked and water had overflowed on it, turning the snow to slush. That's a dangerous situation, common in the forty below temperatures of the North. The slush can freeze in a thin crust on top but is still not safe for travel. I turned the dogs up the steep bank onto the timbered hillside. It meant my going ahead with the jerk line of the toboggan, a twenty-foot length of half-inch rope fastened to the bow, and giving the team a hand.

In ordinary travel the jerk line was allowed to trail behind and if the musher was not steering with the handles of the sled he held it in his mittens so he could jerk the bow to right or left and avoid trees or other obstacles in the trail. Now I'd use it to help pull the load and to hold the toboggan from sliding off down the hillside. I was proving the truth of an old saying among veteran mushers, that when driving dogs with a heavy load the man is the hardest working member of the team.

After a mile of hillside we were able to return to the river ice. It had been grueling hard work holding the toboggan from slithering down the steep hillside, and we were glad to get back to the smoothness of the river ice and find a place to stop and make a fire, boil tea, and rest. By the next day we were in the high country and soon came to Magundy Lake. The lake was crisscrossed with fresh caribou tracks, so we decided to make camp and stop over a day or two while I hunted fresh meat.

As soon as the tent was up and warm, I took off, following the caribou. In a mile I came on them browsing on sparse brush between the hummocks of this windswept plateau. Picking out a young bull, I dropped him with one shot and returned to camp. It was getting late but I hitched up the dogs again and hauled the meat back to camp. We feasted that night on liver and kidneys while the dogs got their fill of fresh meat.

When we left Magundy Lake we followed a small west-flowing creek to its head. Beyond that the plateau was typical high-divide country, low hummocks and frozen swamps so that our trail twisted and turned as it wound its way through the stunted, scrawny spruce trees. We lost track of any worn trail and just kept our direction easterly, hoping to strike Rose Creek which would take us off this barren plateau down to the Pelly River.

The trail got rougher as a strong wind started blowing

and driving a heavy snow in our faces. Joyce slid deeper into the sleeping bag on top of the load so that both she and the baby were completely covered and protected from the cruel wind. I looked desperately about for a place to make camp, but there was no shelter from the increasing storm and no trees fit for tent poles or firewood.

We were in danger!

We had to get into the shelter of heavy timber or we could be frozen to death.

I shouted at the dogs, urging them for more speed, but they were already tired from facing the storm and their eyes were rimmed with ice. Taking the jerk line I snow-shoed alongside them, pulling desperately on the load and encouraging the dogs to stay with it. The wind groaned in our ears as it drifted the snow into every crack and crevice on the toboggan. Darkness fell suddenly, shutting off the sight of the horizontally driven snow, but we could feel the sting of the icy flakes as they drove blackly against us. Somewhere ahead there must be timber, shelter, safety.

I had spent three winters in the wilderness alone and one winter in Juneau where the Taku wind howled up the Gastineau Channel with its driving cold sleet and snow, but I'd never been out on a night worse than this. Had I been alone I might have just snuggled down in my bedroll in the lee of the toboggan, letting the dogs curl up in the snow with their noses tucked under their tails. But I was not alone. The enormous responsibility I had undertaken, to care for a wife and wee son, forced me on.

We fought against the blinding snow that cut against our eyes. Even the dogs pulled their heads down sideways to avoid the worst of the stinging, hissing snow. Snow seethed along the sides and over the top of the toboggan, menacing my loved ones under the robes. The icy wind sucked the breath out of my lungs as I gasped from the heavy exertion of lugging on the rope.

How puny it made one feel fighting against the limit-less power of nature. This was the land I loved, the land of which I had sung such high praises to my bride. Would nature now turn on me, scoffing at my efforts, and snuff out me and my family like a candle? Somewhere out of the dark I became aware of tall shadows—and of the wind whistling and howling high overhead in treetops; now there was no wind, no snow driving in our faces. The moment I shouted "Whoa" to the dogs they just dropped on their bellies, exhausted.

I walked back to the family. The baby was crying; Joyce was comforting him with the nipple of an empty bottle.

I cut a dry tree and started a fire as quickly as I could. Once it gave light, I found more dry trees and dragged them to the fire until I had a huge blaze going. After a while I cut poles, got the tent pitched and floored and the stove in place. Joyce made up a thermos of baby food and fed Syd, while I tied the dogs and gave them a generous feeding. Too worn out to want supper for ourselves, we slid into our bedrolls and were instantly asleep.

We stayed in that camp two days, resting, preparing good meals and doing essential baby laundry, drying it by the open fire. On the third morning we took the trail once more, and soon struck the steep valley of Rose Creek where we had shelter again in heavy timber. For the first time since the storm had struck us I began to breathe easy, not guessing there was more trouble ahead. The trail became steeper, the sled threatened to run over the dogs, and it was more than I could do to hold the load back. At a turn among the trees it slid sidewise, smacked hard against a big spruce and overturned. Joyce and the baby were catapulted off and went rolling down the steep hillside. Luckily the snow broke their fall and they were not hurt, but their outer clothing was so full of snow that we had to strip it off and shake the snow out.

Near the mouth of Rose Creek we met a trapper mushing a fine string of six dogs. He was the first human we had seen since leaving the post at Little Salmon, and we pulled off the trail to make tea and chat. To our astonishment, he told us that he had expected to meet us. At Ross Post on the

Pelly, many miles ahead, he had heard via the moccasin telegraph that we were on the trail. Somehow the word had traveled up the Pelly ahead of us, probably from an Indian trapper who had heard about us at Fort Selkirk or Carmacks. The speed and efficiency with which messages traveled via that moccasin telegraph never ceased to amaze me.

We camped that night on the bank of the Pelly at the mouth of Rose Creek. The ice of the river afforded smooth traveling, and two days later we pulled into the tiny settlement of Ross River Post, where a dozen cabins occupied a high terrace on the bank of the Pelly at its junction with the Ross. Pelly Banks was only three days ahead now.

Roy Tuttle, the Taylor & Drury trader at Ross River, greeted us with the usual warm welcome. Other men found places to keep the dogs, and a cabin was made available to us. The warmth and shelter of four walls would be very welcome.

A Sergeant Tidd of the Northwest Mounted was stationed here with his wife, and they invited us to supper. Mrs. Tidd was the only white woman above the tractor-road crossing on the Pelly, some two hundred miles downstream, and Joyce was the first white woman she had seen for more than a year. Her delight at having a visitor of her own kind was obvious.

We rested there for two days while Joyce did laundry and rested up. I went hunting up the Ross but came back empty-handed, and concluded that this was too close to civilization. There were at least twenty people in the area.

The weather turned mild the morning we left Ross River, making the trail heavy and the going hard. We knew there was one bad spot ahead, the dreaded Hoole Canyon. We camped early at the mouth of a creek below it. The Pelly was so narrow here and the current so fast that it formed whirlpools a hundred feet across in the middle of the river, tumbling cauldrons that never froze. However, there was a shelf of safe ice close to the canyon walls on each side, and we would travel there. We found the shelf rough, and in places it sloped dangerously down toward the open water in midstream. To slide into one of those whirlpools would mean certain death. But I took no chances, and the hazardous going of the canyon (through which no boat could pass in summer) was soon behind us.

The third afternoon after leaving Ross River we pulled into the post at Pelly Banks, where my friend Van Gorder was expecting us. We moved into the police cabin where I had stayed on my visit two years earlier, and through Van Gorder I arranged to hire four Indians with good dog teams to help us freight our outfit to Frances Lake. Each team would haul a load of six hundred pounds. The first two pulled out on Easter morning. We followed with the last two the following day. We found the two ahead of us waiting at Finlayson Lake, with a freshly killed moose.

Two items in our loads gave us trouble and slowed us down. The first was a new kitchen stove that kept getting caught on trees because it was wider than the toboggan. The other was six ready-made window frames, complete with glass panes, protected between sheets of veneer. I had plans for a far better cabin than the one I had built originally at the delta of the Finlayson, and those windows would be needed. But hauling them on a dog sled called for a great deal of care.

On the third day, in a blizzard so thick we could not see Frances Lake, our five teams pulled up to the snug little cabin I had left a year and a half before. It was dry and in order, my stack of firewood waiting where I had left it. Even the dogs seemed happy to be tied again in their old kennels, or maybe they were just grateful to rest after that six hundred and fifty miles of hard winter travel.

I arranged with the four Indians to make a second trip and bring the rest of our outfit, while the snow was still good enough.

When we awoke the next morning the storm had ended. The sun climbed above the sawtooth mountains to the southeast and the view across the lake, white and still under its blanket of clean deep snow, was one to take the breath away.

The journey had been a rough one, rough enough for me but far harder for Joyce, who had never ridden on a dogsled until we drove our team out of Whitehorse that cold March morning.

But now she and the baby and I were home.

Joyce threw her arms around my neck and drew me close. "I love this place," she whispered.

16
THREE AGAINST THE NORTH

For there was only you and I, and you were all to me;
And round us were the barren lands, but little did we
fear.

—*"Little Moccasins"*

The local Indian families, as I had expected, were away on their winter trapping grounds. Joyce and I would have Frances Lake to ourselves until they came back, shortly before the spring breakup.

My first job was to hunt meat and get the fish net working. Joyce unpacked our supplies and carried them up into the cache, arranging everything on shelves so she could find them quickly as they were needed. I cut a long channel in the ice, running out from shore near the mouth of the Finlayson, and set my net where it would be in the river's eddy. The mouth of the river would soon have open water, and I could count on fish being plentiful there.

Once the Indian dog teams had made the second trip from the post at Pelly Banks with the rest of our outfit, I felt free to leave Joyce and the baby and go hunting. I left early one morning, with the dogs, heading for the sheep lick twelve miles above the lake.

The sheep were still there. I spotted a number of them

through my glasses while I was still two miles away. I tied the dogs in the timber and started a stalk, keeping out of sight in the shelter of the trees.

The salt-impregnated clay cliffs of the lick had weathered into a dozen or more cone-shaped pinnacles a hundred to two hundred feet high and covering an area of about a square mile. I got within three hundred yards of the sheep before I had to leave the timber and expose myself. They did not panic at sight of me, but one by one they faded out of sight on the far side of those cones.

Finally I climbed up a shallow ravine until I knew I was above them, and then came out in the open. True to the habits of their kind, the entire band started to climb as soon as they saw me. That is their instinctive reaction at the first hint of danger. But they had been hunted very little if at all, and although they climbed away from me they had no concealment and made no real effort to get out of range. I killed three fat rams in a few minutes.

I skinned them carefully, knowing the skins would be needed for mattresses, and dressed them out. Then I went back for the dogs and the toboggan, loaded the meat and started home. The late-winter dusk was deepening when I drove up to the cabin, and for the first time I tasted the deep satisfaction of returning from a hunt to find an eager and excited wife waiting for me. We had kerosene lamps now instead of candles, and Joyce and I sat up late that night, talking by lamplight about my hunt and the many things strange to her that lay ahead.

It would be another month before I could begin work at the mine, so I put in my time improving the cabin. I made a crib for Syd and lined it with one of the sheepskins that I had stretched and dried. The other two I stretched over a pole bed frame and lashed in place with rawhide. They dried tight and flat, and made a fine, soft, full-sized mattress for Joyce and me. I smoothed off windowsills and a table top, and fashioned attractive odds and ends of furniture from peeled alder and willow trunks and from boxwood and the sheets of veneer that had covered our new windows on the trail. I even made Joyce a fancy dressing table with alder legs and a plyboard top, and promised her a tanned caribou skin cover for it. We had brought a suitable mirror in with us.

I also built a snug outhouse, sheltered in a thick stand of trees about two hundred feet from the cabin, using slabs I had had left over at the sawpit two years before. They were seasoned and dry, and perfect for the walls and roof of the little building. I even cut two boards from a dry cottonwood, shaped and fitted them together and planed them smooth as satin for a seat. No movie star was ever prouder of the baby blue plumbing fixtures in her bathroom than I was of that snow white cottonwood john seat, and Joyce measured up by praising it lavishly.

I had a few tools to work with now, including a handsaw, chisel, and hammer. I still lacked a plane but I had become very expert at substituting a sharp single-bit ax, holding the handle at the right angle with one hand and pushing the butt of the blade with the other. I found I could do almost anything that way that I could have done with a conventional plane. I even finished our outhouse with a small window that could be removed and replaced with mosquito netting for the summer.

Our food supplies were no problem, and we were living well except for a lack of fresh fruit. That would come later in the summer in great abundance, once wild berries started to ripen. In the meantime we relied on dried fruits, apples, prunes, raisins, and peaches.

Everything except our meat and fish was expensive. Freight costs from Vancouver to Frances Lake figured out at twenty-eight cents a pound. Flour that had cost three dollars a hundredweight wholesale in Vancouver rose by twenty-eight dollars by the time it reached us. We were careful to waste nothing.

For pleasure, I hitched up the dogs and took my family exploring around the lake. It was getting late now for ice travel and the danger of unsafe ice, especially close to shore, compelled us to keep to the beach or the woods. We also followed my summer trail up to Half-Moon, where I ex-

Joyce in the spring of 1928.

plained the whole operation of gold washing to Joyce. Everything was double fun now.

When the sap started to run I began felling and peeling trees, cutting them into logs twenty-two and twenty-four feet long. They would season and dry through the summer, be light enough to handle by fall, and I would then begin work on a bigger and better cabin.

I taught Joyce to handle the guns, first to shoot grouse with the .22, then to graduate to target shooting with the .30/06. It was essential that she know how to feed herself and survive, in case some mishap befell me. And I knew that could happen, despite the fact that I took great care in everything I did.

My own transformation from beginner to seasoned and self-reliant woodsman had been a gradual thing, a matter of learning one lesson after another, of completing one task and having it fit me for the next. I had learned the rules as

I went along and I had never felt any concern for my own safety.

But now the situation was different. I was responsible for a wife and baby, and especially until our Indian neighbors were back and could help her, I knew I had to guard against an accident, on the trail, on treacherous ice, with the ax or in any other way. As long as we were three against the North, we'd make out handsomely. But if anything happened to me, Joyce and the baby would be in great danger.

She was an apt pupil. She did surprisingly well with the .22 from the start, although she had difficulty with moving targets such as rabbits on the run, and she learned readily the things I tried to teach her about wilderness survival.

The days grew warm in the spring sun, the thermometer climbing as high as forty above at midday, even though it dropped back to zero and below each night. The snow melted on the lake and open water appeared along the beach, and then wide cracks began to crisscross the ice. The spring breakup was at hand.

And one afternoon four Indian families drove their dog teams up to our cabin on the way to their campground, my friends from two summers before. There were Caesar and his grinning wife and many children; Little Jimmy with his brood of five or six; Oaltal, the simple one, with a fat wife who seemed content with him, probably because he was strong and a capable trapper; finally, Meegan with his stern-looking wife and small children. They had seen smoke rising from our cabin and knew I was back. They had halted their teams, fastened plumes on the harnesses of the dogs and put on their brightest bandannas. They made a fine sight as they drove up.

Joyce came running out to watch, and created an instant sensation. All of the Indian women and children, and some of the men, had never seen a white woman before, and Joyce was almost too much for them to believe. They hurried on to their campground, got the camp set up, and immediately made excuses to come back to the cabin and visit us. One of the teen-age girls ventured to stretch out a hand and touch Joyce's wavy auburn hair. She jerked the hand away as if afraid these long curls would bite, but her eyes were dancing with excitement and she was laughing and jabbering in her own language.

Next Joyce brought the baby out for them to see. By that time Syd had a shock of curly blond hair. He was the first white child any of the women had ever seen, and they crowded around, almost in disbelief.

The four families camped below the cabin for three days, visiting us much of the time. I traded for some of their furs, mink, marten, lynx, fox, wolverine, and coyote, even a few wolf, fisher, and otter pelts. The men agreed to work for me again at the gold digging, when they came back from their spring beaver hunt in June. Then, with no announcement and no fanfare, they were gone, fading swiftly up the rivers that flowed into Frances Lake, each family with its load of camp gear and the younger children loaded into a carryall on the toboggan.

The carryall was an elongated, bathtub-shaped contraption, made of mooseskin, running the length of the sled, fitted inside the long handlebars, with sides two feet high to protect the load from snow and weather. It was standard equipment for the Indians and also for us.

My last chore before breakup was to build a smokehouse for fish and meat. It was eight feet by ten, with four corner posts eight feet high, but the walls of slab extended only halfway up the posts. The upper half and the roof I covered with netting. Inside I fixed a series of racks at a height of eight feet. That smokehouse would take care of the problem of winter dog food and would also provide an emergency supply of smoked whitefish and meat for us.

Breakup came first in the Finlayson itself. The thunder and clash of huge chunks of ice tumbling down through the canyon startled us out of sleep night after night. The ice piled on the beach around the mouth of the river, and smashed its way out into the still-frozen lake for half a mile, grinding and groaning and rumbling.

Now I could go back to gold washing.

Until the Indians returned I'd have to work alone, but I was used to that. I pulled and sweated the sluice boxes

Finlayson Canyon at the upper end of the Half-Moon diggings.

Our claim marker on the Finlayson: "Joyce Lease No. 1 Post."

into place, skidded the lengths of flume to where I wanted them and piled rocks under them and beside them to hold them there. Some of the lumber had warped since I had last worked the mine, more than eighteen months before, but I soaked the boards and straightened them with cross-pieces nailed across the top. At last I was ready to start the summer's work.

It was almost three miles by trail from the cabin to the gold diggings. I walked it right after breakfast each morning, shoveled gravel into the sluice boxes for about eight hours, making tea at noon and eating the lunch I had brought with me. I left Half-Moon in late afternoon, in time to be back at the cabin before dark. One or two of the dogs went with me. The rest I left at the cabin, company and protection for Joyce.

Every evening after supper I tended the fishnet and showed Joyce how to cut and dry the fish. Some evenings we fished from the bank at the mouth of the river with fly rods, for trout. We caught so many whitefish that I finally pulled the net out of the water. We were taking too many for our current use and it was too early in the year to store dog food for next winter. The fish were thin and lacked fat now, after a winter spent half dormant. The fat, full-fed ones of fall would be much better for storage.

Open water extended into the lake for half a mile now, and despite its chill, several times Joyce and I stripped our clothes off and went swimming close to the beach, enjoying the sting of the icy water and reveling in the freedom from convention we had in that far-off wilderness place.

Spring came fast, the sun climbing higher into the north as June approached, the days becoming longer and longer, the nights little more than brief twilight. We planted a vegetable garden in front of the cabin, and then the Indians came back and settled into their camps for the summer.

A strong wind smashed the last ice off the lake on June 10.

The Finlayson was at flood stage, and I had moved my sluice boxes and flume back out of reach of the high water. But I had not moved them far enough. A torrent pouring over huge boulders at the head of Half-Moon carried three lengths of flume downstream overnight and broke them up.

I had no lumber to replace them and I could not afford to delay my gold washing while I whipsawed the boards. It was a minor disaster, but I soon hit on a remedy. I'd tear up the boards I needed from the floor of the cabin. They could be replaced later, by a few evenings of whipsawing.

They were twelve feet long, and although they were dry they still weighed about twenty pounds apiece. Three of them made a sixty-pound load, and that was more than enough. The three-mile trail to the mine ran mostly uphill, between trees part of the way. Each of us (Caesar and Little Jimmy and Oaltal were helping me now) carried our three boards first on one shoulder, then on the other, and finally on top of our heads. We got the job done, but not without some very fluent cussing in both English and the local Tahltan dialect.

As for my Joyce, she had once more proved herself completely the frontier wife. She had not so much as hinted at any objection when I proposed ripping up half the cabin floor for flume lumber. I had certainly picked the right girl.

In the hot sun of the subarctic summer our garden sprouted almost overnight. In three weeks we had lettuce full-headed from seed. Radishes, chard, cabbage, and carrots began to find their way onto the table. And then the wild fruit started to ripen.

I led Joyce to huge areas covered with currants and raspberries. She took one of the dogs and one of the Indian boys with her, as a safeguard against bears in the berry patches, and went picking day after day. The Indian teen-agers were practiced with a .30/30, and as long as she had one of them and a dog along there was little real danger. But once or twice I came home to find that fresh bear sign had scared her off, and she had fled for the cabin.

We did not lack for recreation. In the cool of evening we fished or often went for a long row on the lake. The summer weather stayed fine, with just enough light rain to make the earth smell like the damp woods I remembered in old England. Wildflowers were in bloom everywhere and wild roses by the millions along the lake shore kept the air perpetually perfumed. Sometimes we varied our routine by hiking, but the moss was so soft and deep that we were restricted to the few trails we had available.

I did more work on the cabin, enlarging the window openings to accommodate the six-pane sashes we had freighted in. Mosquitoes were a problem for Joyce and the baby, but bacon fat for her and olive oil for Syd served well as repellents. I had gained a high degree of immunity, simply by letting them bite me at will in the early spring, probably the same procedure that rendered the Indians almost entirely oblivious to the bites. I had never known an Indian whom they really bothered.

One evening one of Caesar's daughters, about eight years old, came to the cabin with an older sister, in tears and holding her left arm against her chest. The hand was a frightening sight, covered with huge yellow blisters. The older girl explained that Oaltal had killed a moose the day before and it had been shared among all the families as was customary. The eight-year-old was helping her mother render the fat over an open fire, and one of her brothers accidentally jolted her. Boiling-hot moose tallow had poured over the entire hand. We had in our first-aid kit bandages and a pound can of ointment for burns. I set the child down at the table, disinfected a pair of scissors and cut away the blisters, exposing raw flesh. Then I covered the hand with the ointment on cotton pads and bandaged it properly. The treatment must have hurt dreadfully, but the little girl hung onto Joyce with her free hand and not a whimper came from her. Finally I put the arm in a sling and told the older sister, as best I could with the little Tahltan I knew and a lot of sign talk, that the bandages must not be disturbed for a few days. I went back to the Indian camp with the two girls, hoping to find Caesar or Little Jimmy and give them instructions. But the men were all away hunting and none of the women spoke any English, so I could only trust to luck and hope for the best.

It was typical of the Indians that they had said nothing to me about going away for a few days to hunt meat. I was alone at the mine for the next three days, and I put in my time cleaning up the sluice boxes. We had been working a rich patch of gravel, and when I panned the concentrate in the bottom of my three sluice boxes I found that a week of washing had yielded about $500 worth of gold, in the form of fine "color" and rough nuggets, some of them as big as my fingertip. To get that twenty-seven ounces of gold we had moved a hundred forty cubic yards of gravel. It had been hard work, but well worth it. We had averaged about $3.50 a yard, a real bonanza, and the thrill of panning that rich concentrate and seeing the bright rim of gold settle along the edge of the black sand was in a class by itself.

I saw the little girl two days after I had bandaged her hand. The sling was gone and the bandages frightfully dirty, but the hand recovered without complications.

The summer fled swiftly. I spent the long sunlit days working at the mine, Joyce tended the garden and helped Syd take his first uncertain steps. We put the net back in the lake and she learned to tend it. She continued to pick gooseberries, raspberries, currants, and, toward the end of summer, blueberries, and converted them into mouth-watering pies. We had some good laughs when we recalled her early efforts at pie-making, when we were first married, and the disasters that had resulted. She was growing as skilled at her work as I was at mine.

I rigged a packsack so I could carry Syd, and some days we took him, and Joyce hiked up to the mine with me and spent the day. Our weeks were an unending honeymoon, blessed by perfect health, the warmest kind of companionship and extraordinary happiness. Being completely isolated and on our own seemed only to heighten our enjoyment of each other. Our marriage, we realized, was as good as a human relationship can possibly be.

I was also getting on better footing with the Indians. The men had come to trust me and count me a friend. I laughed freely at their awkwardness with pick and shovel, and they laughed with equal readiness at my mistakes when I tried to speak their language.

One day Oaltal taught me a new and interesting lesson in survival. At the lower end of Half-Moon the Finlayson flowed smoothly past a cutbank, the water no more than two feet deep, with the slack current in shade most of the day. I had fished there with a fly rod and caught some fine grayling.

Oaltal took me there and we came to the river's edge very quietly, screened by a growth of willows. He leaned slowly and carefully over the water, studied it, and said, "Fish here."

Next he slid on his belly until he lay full length on the bank only six or eight inches above the water. He had stripped to the waist, and he allowed his right arm to slide slowly into the river as far ahead as he could reach. With his hand open and fingers spread, he let the current carry the arm downstream.

When nothing happened, he inched ahead a couple of feet and repeated the performance. This time a grin spread across his face as his hand slid along the side of a fish. He raised it out of the water and dipped it in once more. It drifted with the current, over the back of the grayling. The

Indian made a sudden swift lunge and his thumb and fore-finger closed behind the gills.

It was a method of fishing I had never seen before and it looked easy. But when I tried it the fish slithered out of my grasp and fled. It took much practice before I mastered the trick of letting my hand slide along the body of the fish at the right speed, of grabbing at exactly the right time and in the right place.

Frosts came about the middle of August and by mid-September ice was forming and we had to close down the mine. I paid the Indians off with gold pieces and trade goods, holding the price of the latter to the levels at Lower Post and Pelly Banks, and my crew finished the year well satisfied.

We had another shipment of goods and supplies wait-ing for us at Pelly Banks now. We'd go after them shortly before Christmas, as soon as snow travel was good.

We had been aware for some weeks that one thing bothered our Indian friends. They could not understand my keeping a wife who did not know how to tan mooseskins and convert them into clothing, who was not even able to make moccasins, and who did not carry a forty-pound pack and go along with me when I went hunting. The Indian men had urged me repeatedly to take another wife, an Indian girl who could do these things for me. Part of the time they kidded me about it. We had come to be on close and friendly terms by that time, but as the summer came to a close and they referred time after time to the matter of an Indian wife for me, I realized that they were entirely serious about it. Joyce was a good cook and something of a miracle to them, with her white skin and auburn hair, but she was woefully deficient in the qualifications of a good wife by their standards.

I laughed the suggestion aside, telling them it was not the white man's way to have two wives, but finally the matter came to a head.

Two of the women, Caesar's wife Maddie and Little Jimmy's wife, whose name I have forgotten, came to the cabin one evening with Caesar's fifteen-year-old daughter

Adzina. The three of them stood outside the door until Joyce invited them in, as usual. Inside, they squatted, pulling their long skirts to the floor around them. Joyce made them a pot of tea, and they sat so for a long time, sipping from our white enamel cups, saying nothing. Plainly this was no commonplace errand. They had something of importance to communicate. Both the women spoke a little broken English, learned from their husbands rather than from us. Caesar and Little Jimmy did virtually all of the trading for the Frances Lake band, and at the posts they had picked up adequate though broken English. In addition, I had learned some words and phrases of Tahltan and passed them along to Joyce. We practiced new words every night. So the language barrier between Joyce and the two Indian women was not insurmountable. Finally, to put them at ease, Joyce tried a few sentences on them in Tahltan. They both laughed, and then Maddie broke her silence.

"Adzina tsusliga for skukane clan-eteah," she said. "Adzina stay."

It was a statement rather than a suggestion, and had obviously been decided after lengthy discussion in the Indian camp. Translated, Maddie had said, "Adzina make good wife for fine white man. Adzina will live here."

She went on to explain, in broken English and sign language, that Adzina was fifteen and it was time for her to marry. The word stay, with the inflection Maddie had given it, meant that the girl would come to us willingly and happily, because she wanted to and not because of an order.

It was a somewhat complicated proposal to make across the barrier of limited language, but the meaning was clear enough. When Joyce neither accepted nor rejected the offer, the two matchmakers left, taking Adzina with them. But we were sure we had not heard the end of the matter.

We had no wish to offend our Indian neighbors. And as isolated as we were, with the nearest white at Pelly Banks, I thought it might even be dangerous to turn down what was obviously a generous proposal, unless we could give a good reason. After all, these Indians still believed in witchcraft and medicine men, and what they proposed was entirely in accordance with their moral code. They could easily take offense at our rejection of their offer.

We were encouraged by one thing. The women had called me the "skukane clan-eteah," which meant fine white man. At least they held me in high regard, and for that reason might accept our refusal more readily.

Looking back now, almost fifty years later, at our dilemma and our concern about it, it seems a bit ridiculous. But it was real enough at the time, our location and situation taken into account.

We finally decided on a way out. Through the men we thanked the band and explained that our customs did not permit a man to have two wives, adding that with so many fine friends here at the lake I could trade for skin clothing and moccasins and snowshoes, and so did not need a second wife. It was all done politely and gravely, and in the end everybody appeared satisfied. But I kidded Joyce all through the winter about having passed up the only opportunity I would ever have to be a bigamist.

17
OUR NEIGHBORS, THE GRIZZLIES

I'd like to be far on some weariful shore,
In the Land of the Blizzard and Bear;
Oh, I wish I were snug in the Arctic once more,
For I know I am safer up there!
—"I'm Scared of It All"

We first saw the three grizzlies on a grassy slope beside a little creek that came down to the beach directly across from our cabin. That was in the spring of 1928, a short time after Joyce and I had arrived at Frances Lake. They were an attractive trio. A big silvertip had the most completely silvery pelt I had ever seen on a bear; through the field glasses she had the color of a silver fox, the thick, lustrous fur rippled like molten silver when she walked. Following her up the slope came another large bear, perhaps a three- or four-year-old, then a cub.

There were anthills on the slope and the winter snows had flattened some of them four or five feet across. While we watched, the big silvertip lay down with her head in the middle of what we were sure was a crawling mass of ants. Through the glasses we could see her long red tongue work in and out, presumably licking up ant eggs. But she must have gotten a lot of live ants along with the eggs, for all of

a sudden she stood up, shook her head, and charged off
down the slope and into the icy water of the lake. She
plunged her head under the water, then raised it up and
shook it, like a dog shaking to get dry. She repeated the
treatment for five minutes then lumbered back up the hill
and tried eating the ant eggs again. The smaller one did not
seem to be bothered so much by the stinging of the ants, as
she made no effort to rid her mouth of them. It was a
thoroughly amusing performance to watch.

We named all the animals we saw close to the cabin;
inevitably the big bear was called Silver. Joyce named the
smaller one Emma, because she reminded us of the fat and
rotund Indian woman we knew by that name.

We saw the three bears a few more times during the
next weeks, and then in June another group showed up.
This one consisted of a huge boar, much bigger than Silver,
a large enough sow, a youngster probably three years old,
and to our surprise a small cub, not yet six months old.
It was a most unusual combination. We gave the name
Glahzer, the local Indian word for grizzly, to the huge male,
and Joyce tacked the whimsical name of Petunia onto the
female. Had Joyce known the troubles Petunia was to cause
us that summer, I doubt that she would have used such an
affectionate name.

We first saw this second group walking along the beach
toward the cabin, silhouetted against the sunlit water of the
lake. They were a beautiful sight, but we did not want them
for visitors. I went into the cabin to get my .30/06 just as
the dogs spotted them and set up a terrific commotion,
barking and lunging on their chains. The bears stopped a
moment, then took off into the timber.

Authorities on the habits of grizzlies tell me that male
and female grizzlies stay together only at breeding time, and
then only as long as the sow is in heat. The cubs are born
in the den about late January and come out in early May.
In spite of the fact that the sow seldom leaves the den for
food during the winter she suckles the cub and both come
out of the den healthy and fat. The sow will keep the cubs
with her for two or sometimes three years and does not

breed during that time. The normal breeding season for grizzlies in the southern Yukon is late June. It is not, as some authorities have written, in late summer or fall.

How was it then that this sow had a cub with her and was allowing Glahzer to be around? It was a puzzler. It could be that the cub had just been adopted by the sow. This happens sometimes when a cub is orphaned or gets lost. It was now late June, so it could well be that Petunia was in normal heat. The only other reason I could figure out was that food for the grizzlies was exceptionally plentiful and that they actually lived as a family. I have seen as many as twenty bears, of all ages and both sexes, feeding together on a wartime dump near Whitehorse. Many people have studied the Alaska brown bears feeding on the salmon runs at the McNeil River southwest from Anchorage, where one may see males and females with cubs, all intent on catching salmon and none interfering with others.

It's my belief that if food is sufficiently plentiful and there is no feeling of competition, a sow and boar may live closely during parts of the year, especially in June or during the fall fishing period.

By now it was obvious that we were to have grizzlies for neighbors. How that would turn out I wasn't sure. But I was convinced that it would lead to some lively experiences, and I was right.

I had had my first meeting with a grizzly back in the fall of 1923, when I had been less than six months in the North, and it had been a hair-raising encounter. Arthur Brindle and I had gone down the Stikine from Telegraph Creek that October to examine some mining property that belonged to Groundhog Jackson. One morning while we were at Jackson's cabin, Cap Conover, an old-time trapper and prospector, came down from his place at the mouth of the Clearwater, a short distance up the Stikine, to chat with Groundhog. Before he left he said he was going duck hunting, and invited me to go along. We had three days to wait for the boat back to Telegraph Creek, so I gladly accepted.

We followed a trail along the riverbank to the place where Cap had tied his canoe, and paddled across to his cabin. There we packed a lunch, took two twelve-gauge shotguns and went back to the canoe. We recrossed the river and entered a slow-currented channel known as the Big Slough. It left the Stikine five miles upstream, cut a wide arc around willow flats, and joined the river again opposite Cap's cabin. The flat area above the slough, between it and the mountains, was on the top of a lava bed perhaps two hundred feet above the slough, and was dotted with small lakes, making an ideal feeding ground for ducks. It was used by thousands of ducks when the fall migration was pouring south. Geese as well were on the way to their wintering grounds now, and huge V's of them passed overhead, their distant flight talk floating down to us as we drove the canoe upstream against the slack current of the slough.

We had covered about two miles when Cap pointed to a high point of lava jutting out almost over the water.

"That's my lookout," he said. "Up there I can see all over these flats and spot a moose feeding a mile away. It's easy to get the meat out down here. Beats hunting up in the hills."

A little farther upstream we tied the canoe to a big cottonwood where a trail came down to the water, shouldered our light packs containing our lunch, and Cap led the way up the trail. Less than a mile of hiking brought us out on the lava flats where small creeks meandered from one lake to another, through patches of grassy swamp. The trail we were following stayed on higher ground, and moose runways crisscrossed it everywhere. At a bend in the trail I pulled up short.

"Hey, Cap," I called out. "Look at these bear tracks. They sure look awful fresh to me."

Old Cap took a casual glance at the big sign on the trail, reading it like a book, from his long experience. "Yes," he admitted, "It's fresh, all right. Maybe we jumped him as we came along. Mostly though, these grizzlies won't bother anyone this time of year; they've been fattening up on salmon runs these last two months. They're fat and lazy now."

I respected his knowledge but would have felt a lot more confident if I had brought my .30/06 along. We turned off the trail, walked down to the marshy shore of a small lake and crouched behind a windfall at the water's edge. Almost at once a flock of mallards landed with a splash at the far end of the lake and then another flock came in low, directly over our heads. We dropped four, picked them up and went on to another lake.

We found birds wherever we looked, and when we stopped on a moss-covered bank to eat lunch in the warm afternoon sun, our packsacks bulged with our kill.

"Time to start back," Cap announced when we finished eating. "We'll go back by way of my lookout. Maybe we can spot a moose. If we do, we'll go after him in the morning."

The fall colors along the trail were brilliant, and the wind settled down for the evening as we emerged from the trees onto the lookout. The smooth lava surface jutted out from the timber for about a hundred yards, making a point like a huge V. From the point of the V the lava was broken away, leaving a sheer wall that dropped two hundred feet to a tumbled broken slide that continued down to the edge of the slough. Both sides of the V had these same precipitous walls, so the only way to the lookout point, or back from it, was through the base line of timber and across the one hundred yards of bare lava to the edge of the precipice.

I had shipped a bootful of water retrieving a duck at the last lake and now took the boot off and emptied it over the edge of the precipice where we sat. As I did so, a queer feeling of uneasiness came over me. Some subtle sense of danger made a cold shiver creep up my spine. It was like the shock a man feels when he's out alone and hears the drawn-out howl of a timber wolf. As I pulled on my boot I *felt*—rather than saw—Old Cap reach beside him for his gun. Then we were standing, although I don't remember getting to my feet. I remembered that my shotgun was empty, that the last two shells I had borrowed from Cap were gone.

Together, without a word, we turned toward the timber. I glanced at Old Cap and saw his jaw muscles twitch a little as he held his 12-gauge loosely in front of him. I looked past him to the edge of the timber.

Facing us, blocking our only possible exit, was a massive grizzly sow. Beside her two small cubs stood watching us. One of them trotted out toward us in a playful gallop, like a child's puppy chasing a ball. With a grunt the old she-bear ran out after it and cuffed it with a huge paw, sending it spinning through the air back to the trees. For a moment she just stood there, eyeing us, making me wish for that heavy rifle again. Then she turned and chased her cubs back into the woods.

Cap and I made tracks for the timber farthest from her, but before we had taken ten steps she ripped the evening stillness apart with a bawling roar. With a gasp I turned and saw the huge sow start toward us on the run, her mane bristling over the huge hump above her shoulders, her enormous head hung low and swinging from side to side. She seemed to roll, rather than run, across the open space between us. The silver hide rumpled and stretched over the massive body. She looked as big as a mountain in that hazy light. We backed almost to the edge of the precipice. There was nowhere to run, no tree to climb, and it was impossible to climb down the sheer wall behind us.

I looked at Old Cap. My chance of life lay in his hands.

His face was set. His firm jaw stuck out a little as he watched the oncoming half-ton of fury.

Midway across the open space she stopped and reared up on her hind legs, raising her front legs toward us as if gauging our size. The long curving claws of white ivory glistened their deadly threat. The lighter marking on her chest showed where her heart lay beneath that silvery coat. God, how I wished for a rifle at that moment!

With a bellow the sow came down on all fours and started the final charge. I stood rooted in my tracks, my heart hammering at my ribs. Old Cap did not move. He just stood there, his gun held lightly in front of him, both barrels loaded and cocked, waiting for that red-eyed monster to sweep us into eternity.

Those moments seemed like a thousand years. I could

see the mean beady eyes, the huge slavering jaws. On she came—one hundred feet, fifty feet, thirty. Would Old Cap never fire? I could not believe this was really happening. Slowly the old man raised his gun. Deliberately he took aim and waited. With all the vast knowledge of experience he waited with a terrible patience and nerve.

The bear was almost on top of us when, with a deafening roar, the shot from both barrels smacked into that enormous shaggy head.

Cap and I both jumped aside. The huge beast tried to slew around as the shot, striking like a ball, blinded both eyes. But the impetus she had gained in her mad charge carried her past us, and in a flash she was over the precipice. I heard an agonizing death bellow, followed by the slide of rocks as she struck the broken basalt two hundred feet below.

Without a word we headed for the trees and came down the steep trail toward the canoe. We clambered over the broken lava and came to where the grizzly lay, stretched out over the jagged chunks of dark rock. The whole top of her skull was gone, and blood was streaked along her back. The massive muscles of her front legs hugged a boulder the size of a man.

A hoot owl sounded off in the distance as we threaded our way back to the canoe. Praise beyond words for Old Cap's nerve choked in my throat.

Remembering that experience I couldn't shake off a certain feeling of uneasiness at the idea of having several adult grizzlies around the cabin, but I also thought we could get along with them if we observed their rules. I have always believed it is rare for a grizzly or any other animal to make an unprovoked attack on a human. The attack may *appear* unprovoked, but in the mind of the bear there is a reason for it. A grizzly is so powerful that it has nothing to fear from other animals. Most animals attack others either to make a meal of them or in fear, in self-protection. In spite of the wild stories of bears hunting and downing moose or caribou and feasting on them, it has been my experience that they do not. They will eat a carcass that another animal has killed, but—although most people may not know it—grizzlies are vegetation eaters. I believe that 90 percent of a grizzly's diet is fresh leaves and roots. I have seen patches where wild onions and other bulbous plants grow, dug up for several square yards, where a grizzly has been feeding.

If a grizzly is suffering from an old wound made by a shot she will rightly connect man scent with her pain and reasonably attack. Or, as in the case of Old Cap and me, if a man is too close to her cubs she will take immediate steps to protect them.

When I was in Juneau, during Prohibition years in the States, an Internal Revenue officer was searching for an illegal still in heavy timber and thickets of devil's club. He jumped over a windfall and actually landed on top of a grizzly. The bear's attack was instant and almost lethal. Luckily for the officer, the owner of the still was nearby. He heard the ruckus, came running, and killed the grizzly. Then he carried the badly mauled and injured man to the road and got him to a hospital in time to save his life.

I was hiking on the trail up to the mine one day with my lead dog, Rogue, running ahead of me, when he spotted Petunia on a hillside above the trail, feeding on currants. With far more courage than sense he went barging up the hill at her, barking angrily. I rounded a bend in the trail to see him dodging in and out, daring her to fight. At first she paid no attention beyond raising her head casually to watch him. I yelled to the dog to come back.

Then the grizzly pounced. She must have weighed the better part of half a ton, and it was hard to believe that such a heavy and awkward-looking body could move with such astonishing swiftness. She jumped straight up in the air, like an overgrown cat, then came down on her front feet, missing Rogue by inches. He streaked down the hill toward me, with the bear at his heels. By that time I had had the .30/06 off my shoulder, but I didn't want to kill her. I screamed to scare her off, but when she kept coming I fired a shot over her head. That stopped her for a moment, and when she started to run again she was headed for her two youngsters on the other side of the currant patch. She gave the little cub a cuff that sent him scurrying into the timber ahead of her, and the family went out of sight. Rogue was about as scared as a dog could be, but I doubted that it would cure him. The feud between dogs and bears is too deeply rooted to be erased by one close call.

Hunting grouse one day on the trail up the Finlayson I came across several large trees where bears had been rubbing their backs. They seem to delight in this, especially during the molting season. Clumps of grizzly fur clung to the bark where the bear had been standing up and rubbing its back on the trees. A little farther on I came to a fifty-foot poplar tree. Claw marks had torn across the bark, leaving scars and scratches eleven feet above the ground. Perhaps it is a way of marking off the boundaries of a territory, but I think it is just that grizzlies like to sharpen their claws and stand on their hind legs to do so. This one had to be over nine feet long.

There was another time, at the end of summer, when Petunia and Glahzer gave us a few very uneasy minutes. We were awakened just before daylight by the barking of the dogs. I suspected that a moose might be traveling toward timberline for mating, and I stumbled out into the predawn darkness with the .30/06. I could see no reason for the commotion, but the dogs continued to yelp and leap at their chains. Then, as my eyes got used to the dim light, I saw two grizzlies tearing at our fishnet a hundred yards up the lake. By their size I figured they had to be Glahzer and Petunia. They were out in water about two feet deep, clawing the net ashore, ripping it, and feasting on whitefish.

Joyce came to the door and I told her to stand by with the shotgun. This was a dangerous situation. There is nothing a grizzly is more reluctant to do than give up food it has found, and if this pair decided to make trouble they had only a hundred yards to come. The light was poor for shooting and they could be at the cabin in two streaks. But I couldn't stand by and let them destroy the rest of the net. With spare shells in my hand, ready for instant reloading,

I fired two shots in swift succession close over their heads. They both dropped the net and stood erect on their hind legs to stare in our direction. They were big grizzlies and made a magnificent sight, standing there side by side like two prehistoric monsters. Joyce did the right thing. She lit our Coleman lantern, ran to the door, and hung it on a peg behind me. It threw enough light on the bears that I could have killed both of them, but that was the last thing I wanted to do if it could be avoided.

I sent a third shot whistling over their heads, and that and the light were too much for them. They dropped down on all fours and ran. People and dogs and even shooting they had little fear of, but the bright light of the lantern was beyond their understanding and more than they were willing to face. I fired a final shot over them as they scurried up the beach and into the timber of the delta.

Not all our encounters with grizzlies were scary. Joyce and I were grouse hunting one day, following a trail that ran down the lake close to the beach. A couple of miles from the cabin we stopped to look through our binoculars at a bay. A movement caught my eye, and after watching it a moment I handed the glasses to Joyce. Petunia was lying flat on her back and the little cub was nursing greedily, sprawling its fat little body all over its mother's big belly. The older youngster, far too big for such privileges, kept jumping on his mother and biting at her nipples. She pushed him away with one foreleg and cradled the cub with the other. It was a pretty maternal performance to watch, making it hard to believe that such an animal could be suddenly ferocious and deadly.

That fall, on a goat hunt across the lake from our cabin, I found the tracks of Silver and Emma and to my surprise they now had two cubs with them. There had only been one in the group we had seen in early spring. I camped at timberline that night, and right after breakfast the next morning, glassing the talus slopes and rough peaks above me, I spotted four grizzlies on a high ridge. At first I mistook them for caribou, or perhaps wolves, but before they crossed the ridge and went out of sight I had recognized the sheen of Silver's coat. Curious about what they were up to in that high country in early fall, I climbed after them. From the top of the ridge I located the group again. They were down below me in a small high valley surrounded by talus slopes, digging for marmots. There were marmots all over that valley, their shrill whistling piercing the thin clear air, and the bears were having good hunting. They were clever at it too. While one adult clawed away the rock and earth at the entrance to a marmot den, the other searched out the exit hole that is a standard part of every marmot dwelling, and started to dig there.

We enjoyed our grizzly neighbors that summer. Admittedly, they gave us a bad scare or two, but we probably scared them too with our camp smoke smells, our dogs, and our shooting. Enraged, such a powerful beast can be terrifying, but almost always it refrains from picking quarrels with humans unless they violate its rules. I would sooner trust a grizzly to do what is expected than a weasel or certainly a mink. I have hand-fed weasels, but with a mink that's a chance I wouldn't take.

18
FILLING THE
LARDER

Hist! See those willows silvering where swamp and
river meet!
Just reach me up my rifle quick; that's Mister Moose,
I know.

—"While the Bannock Bakes"

The time had come now to fill the larder in preparation for
the long winter.

Our garden had produced a fabulous crop of vegetables
as summer came to a close, and we were ready to dig and
store the potatoes, carrots, turnips, and onions.

I dug a cellar under the floor of the cabin, a hole ten
feet long, six wide, and four deep, and fashioned a trapdoor
over it of floorboards. The soil was sandy and the digging
was easy. We cleaned the vegetables, put them in sacks that
had held some of our freight from Pelly Banks, and when
the job was finished the cellar was just about filled up. Our
cabbages we left in the ground to freeze. We would cook
them by plopping them into boiling water, unthawed. That
way they would be firm and tasty. Cabbage that has been
frozen and thawed turns mushy on cooking.

We had the net back in the lake, stretched between a
post at the water's edge and a pole driven into the bottom

Joyce's first moose.

fifty feet offshore, held upright like a fence by cork floats and lead weights. Whitefish swam clockwise around Frances Lake, close to shore in shallow water in the fall, and some evenings we caught as many as fifty at one haul. We pulled the net onto the beach, untangled the fish, killed them and then cleaned and split them. They were then hung over the racks in the smokehouse to smoke and dry, and Joyce took on the job of keeping a fire of green willow brush smoldering under them. It took three days for a batch to dry thoroughly. Then we put them in gunny sacks and stored them on the high cache. Our catch through August and September totaled about two thousand, mostly whitefish with a scattering of lake trout. We pulled the net and began to lay plans for a fall hunt.

By that time we had chosen the location for our new cabin, and before the ground froze we dug trenches for the first tier of logs. The logs were waiting now, peeled and dry. As soon as the first snow fell we'd start the job of hauling them from the delta to the cabin site. We were looking forward to that new home as eagerly as any young city couple planning a move into more comfortable quarters.

The start of our hunt turned into a double birthday celebration. Syd's first and my twenty-eighth were only two days apart, and we could think of no better way to honor the occasion. We loaded the boat with a camping outfit and plenty of fresh food, and the morning Syd was a year old we hoisted the sail and started down the lake with a fair wind pushing us along. We had decided to pay a visit to the galena claims up the East Arm and hunt in the mountains above them.

The weather was beautiful and the scenery breathtaking. The high mountains that hemmed Frances Lake were capped with their first snow now, and lower down, along the shore, poplar and cottonwood and willow were decked in glorious fall colors.

We ate lunch without going ashore, and in midafternoon we landed and made camp where the East Arm entered the West Arm, opposite the Indian cabins at the narrows. We had turned the dogs loose when we left our home place, taking only Rogue in the boat with us. The others had run along the beach, keeping abreast of us. They were on the main shore now and we were at the tip of the peninsula that divided the two arms of the lake, so as soon as I had the family safely ashore I tied Rogue, took the boat, and fetched them across.

I tied and fed them, and Joyce and I cooked our supper over an open fire. There could be no happier way to celebrate birthdays.

We sat up late beside the fire, watching the stars come out, listening to the soft lapping of waves on the beach. When we went to our bags silence crept in on us, and the next thing we knew day was breaking and the dogs awakened us with frantic yelping.

I jumped up, grabbed my gun, and ran out of the tent, expecting to see a moose or possibly a caribou crossing the lake, or a bear in the brush nearby. I had by that time developed a sense of smell akin to that of the dogs, so that I could scent big game as far as half a mile off if the wind was right. I smelled nothing and saw nothing, yet the dogs kept barking. Then a twig cracked close by, and I turned quickly. In a spruce tree twenty yards away, a fat old porcupine was edging out on a limb in quest of a bark breakfast. I quieted the dogs and left him to his own affairs.

We started up the East Arm that day, rowing against a bothersome head wind, again putting the dogs ashore to lighten our load. The lower end of the East Arm was a series of small lakes and bays, connected by narrow channels, for eight or ten miles, so the dogs had to run miles around the beach as we rowed from one narrows to the next. But they kept up with us without difficulty. About two in the afternoon the wind freshened and the waves became dangerous, so we went ashore in a small bay and made camp. The dogs came panting in almost at once.

With our glasses we could see goats on the mountains across the lake. We found currant bushes, and while Joyce gathered a bucketful of the ripe fruit, I took the shotgun and hiked to the next bay, where we could hear ducks quacking. I found eleven mallards there, came on them over a low rise of ground and killed four with two shots from the single-barrel Stevens. We left them unplucked, planning to keep them for winter.

The next day we made camp near the head of the East Arm, at the mouth of the creek where the silver-lead claims were, the same place where Amos and I had camped with the Indians three years before. It was an excellent campsite, sheltered by spruce timber, with pure cold water from the creek, and lake trout, whitefish, and pike waiting to be caught from shore. Before we turned in I swung a hook baited with moose meat as far out as I could throw it, and landed a five-pound pike on the first try. Seven casts yielded three good fish. What we did not need we fed to the dogs. There would be no need for a man ever to go hungry in this place.

We decided to camp here while I hunted meat up in the mountains. There were fewer blackflies on the beach, and less likelihood that prowling bears might pay a visit. With the dogs tied in camp, Joyce would be safe enough in my absence. She would have the shotgun and the .22, and it was agreed that if I heard a shot fired I would hurry back. In turn, if something happened to me I'd fire three signal shots, spaced a minute apart, and repeat after five minutes.

Joyce would then let two dogs loose and start for me with Rogue on a chain. The remaining three dogs would stay tied to protect the boy.

The chances of an accident were slim, for I intended to be very careful, but it was only good sense to decide ahead of time exactly what to do if trouble came.

It was a fine morning for a hunt. There was a swampy flat near the mouth of the creek and it had the sour smell of all swamps, but once I gained higher ground that gave way to clean, pine-scented air. Late-fall flowers were still abundant and berry bushes hung heavy with fruit, but a tang in the wind spoke of snow to come. A dozen kinds of small birds flitted in and out of the scrub spruce and willow and alder thickets. Whiskeyjacks came within a yard of me and bluejays shrilled their usual raucous announcement of my movements.

Above timber, at four thousand feet, I sat down and glassed the swampy flats and patches of spruce I had climbed through. The area was laced with moose trails, and presently a movement caught my eye a mile away. Standing with only his head and antlers above the willows at the edge of a very heavy stand of timber, a bull moose was browsing.

I made a big circle all the way back to the shore of the lake to get up on him, shed my packsack, and edged ahead until I was close to the open glade where I had seen him, with the wind in my face. I must have been within a hundred yards when I stopped dead in my tracks.

Standing beside a tree not fifty yards ahead was a huge cow. She was facing in the direction of the bull and had neither heard nor winded me, although I could smell her strongly.

For a minute I debated what to do. If I tried to get around her she would be almost sure to spook and scare the bull off, and I'd lose both. In the end I killed her with a shot through the heart. I heard the brush crash as the bull ran, the noise fading quickly in the distance.

I gutted, skinned, and quartered the cow, covered the meat with the hide to keep flies off, and started down the mountain to camp, carrying the tongue, liver, and kidneys in my pack.

Packing our teakettle and lunch, we started after the moose right after breakfast the next morning, with Rogue, the other dogs following, chained in twos so they would tangle quickly around a tree in case they stampeded at the scent of game. Joyce carried the shotgun, and I had Syd in the packsack I had fixed for him. I also carried the .30/06, in case a grizzly had found and taken possession of my kill. They don't yield their claim easily under those circumstances.

Halfway up to the moose there was a swamp-bordered lake where I had counted about fifty ducks swimming the previous afternoon. When we came to it, we tied the dogs and hung our packs in trees. We wanted some of those ducks.

I don't think they had ever been hunted. I inched up on them, crouched in tall grass, in water halfway to my knees, and they showed no alarm. When I was near enough, two quick shots netted five fat mallards. I built a fire and dried myself out before we went on.

The dogs packed the moose meat down to our camp in three trips, carrying forty-pound loads. They could carry that much since it was a short trip. The nights were cold enough now that we did not need to worry about the meat spoiling. It would freeze hard in three weeks, and would keep until May if stored in shade.

I cut off all the fat for rendering when we were back at camp. It would supply us with cooking fat and "butter" for the winter, and once the meat had frozen it would be given a light coat of the fat to keep it from drying out when the temperatures fell to thirty and forty below. Meat kept that way is as tasty as when freshly killed.

We needed at least one more moose to assure us an adequate supply of meat and fat for the dogs and ourselves for the winter. That one came easy. While we were at breakfast in the tent one morning we heard a splashing down the lake and the dogs broke into sudden yelping. I grabbed the rifle and looked out the tent door. A young bull moose, a two-year-old, was just wading out of the water three hundred yards away. He had swum two miles across the lake to get there. He took one quick look in the direction of the dogs and turned to run.

It was a long shot, but I killed him before he was across the beach.

This was rare luck. He was young and fat and would be prime eating, and I had shot him literally in camp.

Light snow covered the brush and the tent that night. I still hoped to take a young mountain goat, and we needed more ducks, and geese if we could get them.

I hiked away from camp the next morning, with tracking snow in my favor, and climbed through timber laced with moose trails. The moose were near the peak of their rut now, and signs of their lovemaking were everywhere. The bulls had pawed shallow depressions in the ground, two or three feet long. I knew what they had done next. They had urinated in those depressions and wallowed in the mud to scent themselves, and then they were ready to go looking for cows.

I found and followed the tracks of a bull three or four years old. The tracks showed that his hoofs had been rounded off at the point, from his pawing activities. I found where he had bedded, at the edge of a meadow sheltered by timber, and I took the fresh tracks that led away from the bed.

I was approaching a willow swamp when I heard a sudden loud crashing in the brush ahead. I stopped dead still to listen and the crashing noise came again, louder and more prolonged, and I realized what must account for it.

Creeping closer, keeping to a slope above the swamp, I reached a half-open place. I could hear the clash of horns distinctly now and suddenly through the trees I saw what I had expected.

The young bull I had been tracking was standing only thirty yards off. Facing him was an older one, heavier and with a splendid spread of antlers. Both were pawing the

The team pulling tandem toboggans on the East Arm, where I hunted each fall.

ground and uttering hoarse grunts, and the older bull was bleeding from what looked like a deep wound in the right shoulder. Then, a hundred yards behind them, I saw a cow watching unconcernedly.

The young bull took a few steps, lowered his head and made a rush for his rival. The older animal reared, came down, and charged to meet him and they met with a loud crash of horns.

For a minute they wrestled head to head. Then they pulled apart, each trying to rip the other in side or shoulder with vicious swings of his antlers.

The younger one reared to strike with his front hoofs, moose fashion. But before he could start the blow, a tine of the big bull's rack drove deep into his neck and a stream of blood gushed out. The fight was over.

They stood for a moment only a pace apart, not moving.

Then the youngster turned away and staggered slowly downhill, in my direction. His conqueror limped a little, but he strode arrogantly toward the waiting cow, with magnificent pride and antlers held high. As he joined her a second cow stepped out of the brush and sidled up to him, and the three of them went out of sight in the timber.

The young bull was in bad shape, blood spurting from his neck wound. He passed me close enough that I could have hit him with a stone and I spared him further suffering with a shot through the heart.

The next day, while we were after the meat, the sky turned leaden, hinting at a hard storm. The wind came up in the night and at daylight there was six inches of snow on the ground.

We had all the meat we needed for winter now, and with the snow deep in the mountains I decided to give up my goat hunt. We stayed in camp another day and I hunted ducks and crept up on a flock of geese, killing five with three shots.

Our larder was full. We had three moose, more than twenty ducks and the five geese, plus the dried fish, and the vegetables stored under the floor back at the cabin. Two of the geese, we agreed, we would keep for our Christmas and New Year's dinners. We could shoot grouse and rabbits all winter, and take more fish under the ice if we needed them.

It took us two days to get home, but they were clear bright days with the October sun glinting on the water and on the snow-blanketed mountains, and we gloried in the peacefulness and beauty.

It was indeed a happy homecoming. Winter was close now, but we were ready for it. We would start work on our new cabin and the months ahead would be fun—three contented people all by themselves in the wilderness, with everything they needed or wanted.

19
WINTER OF
SOLITUDE

Let the lone wolf-cry all express
Thy heart's abysmal loneliness.
  —*"The Land God Forgot"*

The Indians had scattered to their traplines now. Joyce and the boy and I could expect to be by ourselves, without neighbors, for the next five months.

I carried sand from the beach and banked the cabin to a height of a few inches above the floor. We gathered big piles of moss, and used some of it to repair the chinking. The rest would go onto the roof of our new cabin later on. I had made a caulking tool from a slab of birch, and with it I drove fresh moss between the logs and into the tiniest cracks around the door and windows, knowing that when our thermometer fell to forty below the smallest aperture would let the bitter wind come whistling through.

Then for two weeks I sawed firewood, in temperatures of ten above to twenty below. At the end I had a ten-cord pile, enough for most of the winter. Rim ice crept farther and farther out into the lake, decorated with frost crystals like a meadow of ghost ferns, pygmy size.

One day in early November the sky clouded over and a cold wind out of the north shook the last leaves from the

The new cabin under construction; our high cache is visible behind the tent camp on the beach.

trees. Snow came with it, and at dark the first blizzard of the winter was upon us. It heaped huge drifts around the cabin and along the beach, but Joyce and I stayed snug and warm in the cabin. Then the storm ended as abruptly as it had begun, in the night, and we awoke to a world of unbelievable stillness and beauty.

The snow was deep enough now for hauling the logs from the delta for our new cabin. There were about fifty to be brought in, forty for the walls, the rest for gable ends, ridge, and roof beams. With Joyce as a passenger, we broke and packed down a quarter mile of trail until it was hard and slick, and started the job.

We had peeled the logs as we cut them, back in the summer (Joyce had become very proficient with an old-fashioned drawknife), and smoothed off the knots. Each log had been rolled onto poles to keep it off the ground. They

were dry now and weighed no more than half their green weight.

We skidded them home one at a time, lashing one end to the front of the toboggan, letting the other end drag in the snow. They made heavy loads, but it was a short haul and the dogs made little of it.

We managed to notch and lay one round of logs a day, and the cabin walls took shape quickly. I planed boards smooth with the ax for the door and window frames, holding the logs in place at the openings with wooden pegs.

When the walls reached window height it became too risky to roll them into place on skids. I had a couple of near-accidents, and then rigged a tripod in the middle of the cabin, hung the blocks and tackle I had brought in, and swung the logs up.

For a few days after the storm the weather stayed mild.

Then one night the thermometer fell abruptly to thirty-five below. Trees cracked like pistol shots as they froze and split. Slush ice in the Finlayson jammed and froze, and the rim ice in the lake became safe for three hundred feet out from shore.

I cut a long slot and sunk fifty feet of weighted line into deep water. By keeping open holes at both ends of the line I could run a net under the ice all winter and we would enjoy the luxury of fresh fish whenever we wanted them.

I had not expected to see anything of our Indians until spring, but to my surprise, one morning in early December we saw two dog teams crossing the ice at the mouth of the river, headed for the cabin. It was Little Jimmy and Oaltal. They told me they needed more tobacco and tea and sugar, and they wanted jawbone (credit) until they brought in the winter's catch of furs. I knew they were testing me, but I had nothing to lose, since they would be working for me at the mine again the next summer and could repay the debt out of their wages. I gave them what they asked for, entered the transaction in my account book in trading-post fashion, and they took off along the rim ice. We saw their camp smoke for two days, then they were gone.

We knew we had several hundred pounds of supplies waiting for us now at Pelly Banks, but we were not yet in need of anything and the snow would be better for hauling around Christmas. We decided to finish the new cabin first, and move into it. We would use the old one as a storeroom and trading post for my dealings with the Indians.

Joyce started to practice mushing the dogs by herself, taking two at first and then adding one at a time as she grew accustomed to driving them. If they ran away she could jump off and they would tangle their harness on trees or brush and pile up before they went far. Her greatest difficulty was in harnessing them. They were strong and enthusiastic, jumping and pulling in their eagerness to get going. More than once they knocked her sprawling in the snow.

One morning we saw what appeared to be a band of caribou trotting along the beach at the mouth of the Finlay-

Joyce practicing with the dog team.

son. The glasses showed them to be a pack of seven wolves instead, coming unconcernedly toward the cabin.

The wind was blowing down the lake from the north, so that neither the wolves nor our dogs caught each other's scent. The leader of the pack was a huge black male, trotting proudly ahead. One of the others was rusty red. She was the mate of the black leader. The rest, younger animals, were typical gray.

They came within six hundred yards, and then they must have noticed the cabin smoke wreathing up from the chimney. They pulled up short and stood looking our way.

We didn't want them making their rounds close by, for if nothing else, wolves are dangerous neighbors for sled dogs, so I fired a shot over them. The leader jumped, swiveled around in the air, and the whole pack fled for the timber.

That night, in the stillness of the winter dark, we heard them howling. The wilderness has no sound more beautiful, or more haunting or stirring to human ears. The long-drawn-out musical notes woke us from deep sleep and we lay and listened to the wild chorus, enchanted, yet shivering at the wildness and loneliness of it.

Beginning in a low key, the poignant music rose in perfect harmony through weird half tones and full-throated notes until it reached a crescendo of high-pitched wailing. It was as if the wolves were lamenting their solitude. Then the chorus slid slowly down the scale, full of sadness, to the lower notes again. It sounded like a song of ghosts from a lost legion.

I have always thought that wolves are the most misunderstood of all wild animals. They mate for life and live as a close-knit family, with a leader whose authority is respected on the trail, while hunting, or in feeding. A pack is usually one family, rarely numbering more than eight or nine. Each pack has its own hunting ground, patrolling it and scenting the boundaries to warn other wolves to keep out. Powerful travelers, they cover surprisingly long distances.

It's the old wolf, forced to leave the pack when he is no longer able to fight off a challenger, that is the most troublesome. Hunting by himself, after a lifetime as a member of a skilled team, he can no longer kill moose or caribou. He falls back on rabbits and marmots, takes ducks and geese on their nests, and he is the wolf that may come to a cabin to steal or even attack a chained dog just outside the door.

We would see this pack frequently as the winter went along, crossing the ice, coming from down the lake and disappearing in the timber near the mouth of the river. But they gave the cabin a wide berth, keeping a good half mile away.

Six weeks after we laid the first round of logs we had a beautiful new cabin completed except for the interior. The final and hardest part of the job had been the roof. Once the ridgepole and four heavy roof beams were in place, I dismantled the tripod I had used to hoist the logs up. Then I laid roof poles from the ridge down to the side walls, with a generous overhang, and together Joyce and I covered them with a layer of moss a foot thick. There was no sod available. We had to use moss and gravel instead. The work of hoisting up enough gravel, a bucketful at a time, to cover the moss to a thickness of six inches seemed endless. But it was finally done and the gravel was tamped firmly in place. For a time it would leak and have to be patched, but eventually it would compact until it was watertight and in summer flowers would grow in it.

I laid floor joists, poles resting on the ground, and started to whipsaw boards for the floor. The cabin was twenty-two by twenty-four feet, and the whipsawing was a long hard chore, but I made steady headway.

We were working hard and living a simple, almost primitive, frontier life, but we were very happy. Syd, more than a year old now, was growing fast, eating almost everything, thriving on a diet that included the dry whole milk we had brought in in fifty-pound drums—and also moose steak cooked very rare. He was a strong and healthy little boy with curly golden hair, beginning to talk, big enough to haul himself up on benches and get into everything. He enjoyed being outdoors, even when the temperature was well below zero, and we found him a sheer delight.

I had taught Joyce to set snares for rabbits. I made a small sled for the boy and she took him along when she made her round of the snares. One day we put him in a warm sleeping bag and drove the dogs across the delta to the mouth of the Finlayson canyon, where two winters

The new cabin at Frances Lake built entirely by myself.

before I had watched an otter family at play. They were
still there, and Joyce enjoyed their happy and incredibly
graceful antics as much as I had.

We were having fun as a family, and there could not
have been any more contented people anywhere.

A week before Christmas, again to our surprise, Caesar
and his family arrived at their campground a mile below
the cabin. One of his boys had cut his foot with an ax some
time before. The wound had not been kept clean and now
the foot was infected and swollen painfully. Joyce and I
treated it as best we could, opening the cut, soaking the
foot in water as hot as the boy could tolerate, and putting
on a poultice.

The family's arrival was greatly to my liking. I had
wanted to make the trip to Pelly Banks and arrange to have
our supplies freighted to our place, but I did not want to
take Joyce and Syd along and neither was I willing to leave
them alone. I talked it over with Caesar, and he agreed to
stay close by and let my wife take care of his boy's foot,
while I made a quick trip to Pelly Banks Post. He would
not go there, he told me, because it was outside his tribal
hunting grounds.

I started before daylight the next morning, carrying
only my bedroll, rifle and an extra pair of snowshoes on the
toboggan, driving all the dogs. I reached the post by noon
the second day, having made the seventy-five miles over a
rough trail in a day and a half. I made a deal with the trader
to send Indian drivers with six-hundred-pound loads of my
freight as soon as they came in from their traplines. I loaded
six hundred pounds on my own toboggan, got an early start
the following morning and was back at our cabin at dusk
on the second day. It had been a fast trip, but I was eager
to get home. Christmas was only two days off.

The Indian boy's foot was much improved, the swelling
almost gone. To Caesar this was wonderful "medicine," by
which we knew he really meant witchcraft. It would go far
to cement our growing friendship and respect for each other.

Caesar was the kind one of his band. A mild-mannered
man of about forty, he took in any child who was orphaned

Joyce and Syd in front of the cabin at Frances Lake, Christmas Day, 1928.

or deserted, as sometimes happened. He had fourteen in his family that winter. His happy, wide-grinning wife made them all welcome, too.

Joyce and I had a wonderful Christmas. The day broke clear and cold and we made it as festive as possible. We had presents hidden for each other and Syd. My big surprise for my wife was a gift of a Belgian .410 gauge double-barrel shotgun, a lightweight, beautifully made fire arm that was the pride of my heart. Joyce was completely delighted.

Our Christmas dinner consisted of a roast goose, wild cranberries dug out from under the snow, a plum pudding Joyce had made from dried fruit, and a pumpkin pie. The pumpkin was the only item that came from a can. We had brought in small candles for birthday cakes. They now decorated the Christmas tree, a small spruce I had cut, along with strings of cranberries and cotton wool from our first-aid supplies. Our little cabin (the new one was not quite ready) glowed with warmth and happiness.

In the afternoon we went for a snowshoe tramp across the river, letting the dogs run loose, a privilege they didn't often have. We came home at dusk to the comfort of the cabin and talked of friends and families Outside, wondering with a touch of melancholy how they were celebrating Christmas back East and across the sea in England.

The next day Joyce showed some of the Indian boys her new shotgun. They all wanted to shoot it. I told them to bring their .22 rifles and we would go grouse hunting on the delta. We hunted for an hour, killed several ptarmigan, and I finally told one of the boys he could fire my 12-gauge single-barrel instead.

He shot at a flushing ptarmigan and killed it, but the gun all but kicked him off his feet and that ended the requests to test Joyce's. Back at camp, I let the boys keep the birds, and they had an exciting story to tell of their experience with "the gun that shot many bullets."

Soon after Christmas four Indians arrived with their teams from Pelly Banks with the rest of our supplies. What we could not store in the high cache we put in the old cabin. The new one was complete now except for a few floorboards, so we moved our furniture and stoves in, heated it up, and that night we slept in it for the first time. Compared with the old one, it was roomy and luxurious.

By now the other Indians had come in, including Oaltal and Little Jimmy. I traded cheap jewelry and dress goods for their mink and marten pelts and a few lynx, and the next morning the whole band departed, making a colorful spectacle as one dog team after another crossed the lake, pompons waving from the top of each dog's collar and bright ribbons streaming from the harnesses. It was safe to assume we would not see our neighbors again until breakup.

The cold grew more intense as the New Year approached. Two days before the end of December the thermometer plummeted to seventy below zero! The air was so still that the slightest sound echoed. The commotion of red squirrels chasing one another up trees, or bluejays scolding over scraps of food outside the cabin window, rang loud and startling in the silence.

I piled up extra wood and we kept to the cabin. When I went out the snow crunched under my snowshoes as if I were walking on soda crackers. The sky stayed intensely clear and at night the stars were exceptionally brilliant, appearing closer than usual. Their silvery light only seemed to add to the bitter cold.

The temperature stayed below the minus seventy mark for a day, and at night it dropped to seventy-five. The extreme cold was making life difficult for Joyce and the baby. To use an outhouse two hundred feet from the cabin was a winter hardship that they had tolerated, but now it became downright dangerous. Flesh exposed at seventy below freezes almost instantly. Syd had a white enamel pot, and it had to replace the trips outside for both of them.

New Year's day dawned clear and silent, with the cold unbroken. Our spirit thermometer, hanging free of the cabin wall in front of a window, was calibrated to register down to eighty degrees below zero. That morning we could not read it because of frost.

I dressed warmly, put on my parka, closed the wolverine fur of the hood around my face, and stepped outside for a look. The red liquid had dropped into the bulb, about four degrees below the lowest reading. That meant a temperature of eighty-four degrees below zero! It was by far the coldest day I had ever seen.

The temperature stayed below the eighty mark for three days, even during the daytime. I went outdoors only long enough to split a little wood, and even that posed the danger of frosted lungs, despite the protection of the fur-rimmed parka hood. As soon as I began to feel the chill of that terrible cold in my chest I took refuge in the cabin.

We felt some concern about the dogs. Each had a well-made kennel with a canvas flap, and was chained to a post four feet in front of it. They were naturally clean, incidentally, and their piles of excrement were made at the extreme end of a six-foot chain, remote from the kennel.

How would they fare in such cold? Our worries were groundless, and we laughed as often as we looked out at them. Each dog was curled contentedly in the snow *on top* of his kennel, his nose tucked down in the shelter of his tail, frost covering the rest of his head.

I fed them fresh meat instead of fish while the cold

spell lasted, and let them run loose two at a time. They appeared not to care one iota about the low temperatures.

The cold broke at last and clear sunny days followed one another through January. We settled ourselves in the new cabin and built more furniture and shelves. Snow piled deeper and deeper on the roof, so that we had to brace the ridge pole with posts.

I had notched spreader poles like ceiling joists at the top of the side walls, five feet apart, to keep the walls from spreading out under the weight of the roof. Now we divided the cabin into three rooms by hanging lengths of cloth from those poles.

Our only source of water was a waterhole I kept chopped open in the lake. I had broken a trail from the cabin across the beach and about two hundred feet out on the ice. By midwinter the ice had become five feet thick and I had to cut steps in it to get down to the water safely. I kept open a hole about two feet in diameter, covered with a frame of boards, partly to keep it from freezing over quickly, partly to make sure that Syd did not toddle out on the lake and fall in.

He delighted now in following my snowshoe trails, and he had given us one bad fright when he wandered by himself down the trail to the outdoor toilet and fell in deep snow just off the trail. We missed him, searched frantically, and found him there, too smothered in snow to get back on his feet but none the worse for the experience. We pulled him out, shook and pounded the snow out of his garments, and his mother carried him laughing and delighted with himself back into the cabin.

Two pails of water stood always on a bench back of the stove. We heated what we needed in buckets. For baths we used a washtub that also served for doing laundry. It had one drawback. It could be emptied only by carrying the water outside a bucketful at a time.

What little garbage we had we dumped where we poured the waste water. When the ground thawed in the spring I would bury it.

We had shot two caribou from the first herd we saw crossing the lake in December, but had fed most of the meat to the dogs. Now we found ourselves craving a change from moose meat and fish.

For days I watched down the lake for signs of caribou with no luck. Then one morning I saw a herd of about thirty come out on the ice three miles away. I rushed to harness our three fastest dogs, slid a pair of snowshoes under the loose lashings of the toboggan, grabbed my .30/06, and raced for the caribou, riding on the tail of the sled.

The dogs knew it was a hunt. As soon as I let the jerk line loose from the stump they leaped away down the sloping beach and out onto the lake ice. Shouting to them to "Gee" at the forks of my trail, they swung right and galloped downlake parallel to shore. After a half mile they steadied down to a fast trot. I could see the caribou now, stringing out across the lake, unhurried. Maybe fifty or more were already on the ice and more were following out from the timber on shore. The dog's tails were held high, curled over their backs and wagging furiously, while every once in a while an excited yelp broke from one or the other of them. The hickory boards under my feet fairly bounced on the rough ice and drifts of snow, while I kept a tight hold on the jerk line in one hand, the gun in the other, and kept my knees bent as I leaned forward to keep my balance, like a skier on a long downhill run.

Now I could see the big antlers of the caribou glistening in the sun, while the white rings around their necks and their white rumps faded their outlines against the snow. After another mile the dogs caught the scent of the caribou and instantly went crazy. They yelped and barked in mad excitement, roaring over the ice and trying to pass each other to gain the lead. The whip of the wind in nearly forty below zero stung joyously in my face, pulsating the blood through my veins as the thrill and frenzy of the dogs coursed through the team and washed into me—until I was a part of them. The dogs, unconscious now of the load behind them, leaped through the air in their hunger to get at the beasts, galvanized into magnificent action as they streaked for the caribou.

Now less than half a mile away, the caribou turned toward the sound, standing still and facing the strange onslaught. At last the herd broke. Those in the lead, almost halfway across the lake, herded together. The last, coming out of the timber on shore, clustered into another band, while about twenty beasts directly ahead of us bunched up, making a weaving, milling target.

Commands from me made not the slightest impression on the dogs now, as the scent of raw meat assailed their nostrils: they reverted back through a thousand years of breeding, behaving like a hunger-crazed pack of wolves.

We got to about three hundred yards before the herd sensed their real danger. Then, with snorts and lunges, they whirled toward the shore. I leaped from the toboggan, sprawling in the snow, then rolling to one knee, I pumped a shell into the breach and fired. My hand must have been shaky after the tense ride, for the big bull I sighted staggered but did not fall. I shot again, more carefully, then turned to down two more before they stampeded. The dogs made straight for the first caribou to fall. Disregarding their tangling harness, they piled into it, ripping the underside skin like paper, and getting into the raw meat.

Coming up to the other two I saw that one was still alive, though crippled in his back or hind quarters. Desperately he raised his head, trying to get up on his front legs. I had emptied the five shells from the magazine and now realized that, in my rush to get going from the cabin, I had forgotten to slip a box of extra shells into my pocket. Taking out my sheath knife I studied him a moment. If he could get at me, he could still strike a death blow with those sharp front hoofs. I took a quick chance. Coming up over his shoulder from behind, I jumped and straddled his back. As I did this, I grabbed his nose with my left hand, jerking his head back with my fingers inside his nostrils. As he reared up I slashed the keen edge of the knife across the white throat and leaped clear. My knife cut through the heavy fur and blood spouted from the jugular. In a moment he lay still.

Going over to the dogs, I stripped off their harness and let them eat the waste while I gutted and skinned out the animals there on the ice. I loaded up the three carcasses, covered them with the hides, then harnessed up the dogs again and headed happily for home.

I sang to the dogs as they pulled steadily over the trail we had made coming down. It had been a glorious and thrilling day for all of us. We got back to the cabin well before dark, and after tying the dogs to their kennels, I sat down with Joyce to enjoy fresh caribou liver and home-grown onions.

The rest of January and February passed quickly and the March storms were not too severe. The sun climbed higher in the south now, lengthening the days. I spent my time getting ready for the summer work, cutting enough wood to last until fall, repairing the gill net, driving new caulking into the seams of the boat, sawing lumber and, while the ice was still good on the river, hauling extra lumber up to the mine.

In early April we loaded the tent and camping equipment and mushed north to the sheep lick, planning a combination sheep hunt and camping vacation. It was good for Joyce to get away from the cabin now and then, and she enjoyed camping as much as I did.

We made camp in the timber, out of sight of the lick, flooring the tent with a thick soft carpet of spruce boughs. Temperatures were rising above freezing by noon almost every day now, and I enjoyed hunting stripped to the waist. As soon as the sun sank below the hills, however, cold swept over the land like a blast from a glacier, the thermometer plunging from forty degrees above to fifteen below in a single hour.

The first day I saw only a ewe with two yearlings, but would not kill her, since she would soon be having a lamb. The second morning at daylight I spotted, through my glasses, several sheep coming down to the lick from a higher altitude. I gave them time to get interested in the salt, came out above them and looked them over. There were seven rams in the band, some licking the salty clay, others lying down close by.

I picked the three I wanted and killed the first with one shot. The rest, not knowing where the sound of the rifle had come from, climbed toward me and I picked off the other two.

We headed for home the day after that with a fine load of sheep meat.

In a few days the Indians came by on the way to their annual beaver hunt. They would be back in June as usual, they told me.

Slush and water covered the lake, the river broke and piled huge blocks of ice on the beach. We had seen it all the year before, and knew what to expect. I set the flumes and riffle boxes in place and began washing gold from the canyon gravels as soon as the water started to run.

The Indians came back for the summer and I used up most of our trade goods in exchange for their furs, choosing the smaller pelts that would not make a bulky load to take out by dog team. Joyce and I were planning a trip Outside now, but we would not leave until the following March, when sled travel would be at its best.

Caesar worked steadily at the mine that summer, Little Jimmy and Oaltal and Meegan took turns. It was becoming harder to find rich pay dirt but we were still recovering enough gold to make the work worthwhile.

We had one encounter with a grizzly that summer. Joyce and I were hiking up to the benches above the Finlayson, with Syd in a packsack on my back and several of the Indian kids tagging along. Suddenly Billy, the boy whose foot we had treated, cried, "Skukane, Skukane, glahzer! Glahzer stcho!" (White man, white man, grizzly! Big grizzly!)

He was pointing to a hillside just ahead, bare of trees but covered with wild gooseberry bushes. An enormous fat grizzly was licking the fruit off, moving slowly from one bush to the next, stretching his neck out and guzzling the berries with obvious relish. We could see his long red tongue working and as often as he had his mouth crammed full he raised his head to swallow.

I was carrying my .30/06 as I always did, as a matter of sensible precaution. I told the Indian youngsters to shout in unison when I gave the signal. I bolted a shell into the rifle, said "Now!" and they all yelled.

The bear was surprised but certainly not alarmed. He swung his head to study us and before he could make up his mind to pick an argument, if that was what he intended, I sent a soft-nosed bullet just over his head. That did it. He took off at a rolling gallop.

We closed the mine down in mid-September, with the arrival of freezing weather. By then we had a really good stake. Caesar's wife Maddie had made pokes of tanned mooseskin for us. We had seventeen of them stacked in the cabin now, from our two summers of work, and as nearly as we could calculate each one contained nearly a thousand dollars' worth of gold. We'd go out well heeled indeed.

Our garden produced well again, and we stored the roots in a hole under the floor of the new cabin. We netted and dried the usual two thousand whitefish, and made our fall hunt up the east arm of the lake, taking two young goats and three moose. We also shot all the ducks and geese we wanted, finding them easier to hunt than they had been the autumn before, mostly because we knew just where to look for them.

Syd had learned now to ride on Rogue's back, hanging onto the dog's collar with both hands, and they both seemed to enjoy it. Rogue was six years old and trustworthy, and obviously loved the boy. I no longer had to pack Syd on my back when we went on trips.

The winter passed smoothly and swiftly. As Christmas approached I made a trip out to Pelly Banks and hauled in the supplies we had ordered earlier.

The Indians came at Christmas, and when they left we told them we would be gone before breakup, but planned to return in a year. We stored our leftover supplies on the high cache, braced the cabin roof with extra stanchions, and by the middle of March when the sun was swinging north once more and a heavy crust had formed on the snow we were ready to leave.

We were eating supper our last night in the cabin when my wife, forever full of surprises, said casually, "You're going to be a father again, darling."

On that happy note we took our departure at daybreak.

20
OUTSIDE!

Now I've had my lazy supper, and the level sun is gleaming
On the water where the silver salmon play;
And I light my little corncob, and I linger, softly dreaming,
In the twilight, of a land that's far away.
— *"The Rhyme of the Remittance Man"*

Joyce and I had known, all through the summer of 1929, exactly what we wanted to do. We were eager to see our families again, hers in Rochester, New York, mine in England, and show off our son. We'd book passage for England, come back and stop in my wife's home town, spend the entire summer visiting. We expected to return to Half-Moon late the following winter.

Little did I think, when we closed the cabins and drove the dogs away that bright March morning, that I would not see the place again for six years.

I had loaded the toboggan the day before and checked the load carefully. The seventeen pokes of gold were on the bottom, then the bales of fur lashed down between the long handlebars that slanted up from the forward end and overhung the stern at the right height for a man to hang onto and jog along behind. I had two hundred and fifty pounds of dried whitefish in sacks at the front of the mooseskin

227

On the river trail.

carryall, the silk tent and grub box jammed under the curve of the high bow. A small box of dried food and the little sheet-metal stove with its telescoping pipe made up the rest of the load. Our two sleeping bags lay on top of the furs. Joyce and Syd would ride there. Her snowshoes and my two rifles, the .30/06 and the .22, were under the forward lashings, readily accessible.

Joyce climbed into the carryall and settled Syd on her lap under the robes while I hitched the dogs to the toboggan. It was a fine morning for the start of our long trip out, clear and crisp. The bright sun of late March struck the mountains across the lake, backlighting the snowy peaks in golden flame, and causing the lake to sparkle like an enormous field of gems.

When everything was ready, and the dogs were barking and whining in their eagerness to go, I loosed the jerk line of the sled from the hitching stump and shouted "Mush, Rogue!" The leader lunged into his collar and the five behind him, Rascal, Runt, Scotch, Brandy, and Whitey, the reliable

old bitch that had whelped Rogue, Rascal, and Runt (she was in the shaft position), tightened their traces and we were away.

I headed them onto the trail that led up the Finlayson and Joyce and I turned for a last look at the cabins we had called home for two wonderful and happy years.

Ahead of us lay six hundred fifty miles of sled travel, out to Whitehorse. We were reversing the journey we had made two years earlier.

There would be no packed trails to follow for the first part of the trip. We would go up the Finlayson to the lake of the same name, over the divide and down to Pelly Banks Post. From there we'd mush down the Pelly to Fort Selkirk where it flowed into the Yukon, then up the Yukon and the Nordenskiold to our destination.

If weather favored us and snow conditions stayed good, I knew we might make as much as thirty to forty miles a day, but I figured an average nearer twenty-five. With luck we'd be at Whitehorse in three weeks or a little longer.

The dogs were in top shape and I had all I could do to keep up with them on my small trail snowshoes, hanging onto the jerk line and trotting behind the toboggan. We were almost at Finlayson Lake the first night.

Camp chores on the trail were far easier for me now than they had been when we mushed in to Frances Lake two years before. For one thing, a little boy two and a half years old is much better suited to winter dogsled travel than a baby of six months. For another, Joyce was used to the wilderness now, and was a great help in making camp as well as doing all the cooking.

We awakened at daylight. I lit the tiny stove in the tent and while she got breakfast I broke camp, loaded the toboggan, checked every item, harnessed the dogs, and packed the grub box. We mushed out as soon as we had eaten, carrying thermos bottles of soup and hot milk for our noon meal. We traveled until close to dark. Our days were seventeen to eighteen hours long, but we made fast time.

We reached Pelly Banks as the sun was sinking below the mountains in the southwest the second day. Van Gorder welcomed us and gave us the use of the unoccupied police cabin we had used before.

We traveled thirty-five miles down the Pelly the next day. We were keeping a tight schedule, but we took tea breaks whenever anyone felt cold and rested the dogs after each tough place on the trail. Deep drifts made travel hard in places, and there were stretches of the river where fast water had frozen to form rough ice, with sheets thrown up vertically and snow drifted in between.

Nearing the Hoole River late that afternoon, we came to our first glare ice. The wind had swept a long straight stretch bare, the surface had melted in the sun and frozen at night. It was as slick as glass and the dogs couldn't keep their footing. They slid and skidded. I had to take off my snowshoes, but even my moccasins slipped badly as I helped the team pull the toboggan off the ice and onto snow on shore.

We passed through the Hoole Canyon the day after that. It was a place we dreaded, rock strewn, with water too swift to freeze and a right-angle turn halfway through. There was a shelf of rough but safe ice along the rock wall on either side, but those shelves sloped treacherously toward the big whirlpools where giant ice blocks swirled endlessly, a hundred yards offshore. We hugged the south wall, picking our way between sloping cakes of ice, and shuddering a little at the thought of those open whirlpools. But we made it safely, and once we were on smooth ice again at the mouth of the canyon we went ashore and made camp, exhausted from struggling with the loaded sled on the rough shelf ice.

Long before dark on our fifth day we drove the dogs up the steep bank of the Pelly at the Ross River Post of the Taylor & Drury Company. We arrived in a clamor of barking dogs. Roy Tuttle, the trader, hurried out to greet us and four or five other men gathered around immediately.

Here, on the way to Frances Lake in March of 1928, Joyce had gotten to know the wife of Sergeant Tidd, the Northwest Mounted Police officer stationed at the post. She and her husband were still there. She was the first white woman Joyce had seen in two years, and Joyce was the first she had seen in more than one year. Theirs was a happy and excited reunion.

We laid over a day at Ross River. Joyce and Mrs. Tidd had a thousand things to talk about. Syd played with the Indian kids, and the three of us luxuriated in hot baths and clean laundry, and enjoyed homemade pies and other treats we could not have on the trail. The dogs got a good rest, too, after five days of hard travel.

When we pulled out at daylight two days after our arrival, to our surprise we found a freshly broken snowshoe trail leading downriver for about three miles. One of the men at the post (there were eight white men there, all trappers and prospectors except Tuttle and Tidd) had broken that trail to give us a good send-off. We never found out who the Good Samaritan was, but that little act of kindness was typical of the place and the hardy breed of men that peopled it. Rough and strong, yet slow to anger, there was not one of them that would not give a stranger in need the shirt off his back.

Although the sun was melting the surface of the snow at noon now, temperatures fell to fifteen to twenty below each night. The crust stayed firm and in the mornings I was able to jog behind the toboggan without snowshoes, or even ride for a few miles.

The dogs pulled with a will, yelping in their eagerness to get away as soon as it was light, trotting with their tails curled high, and in the cold, crisp air of the mornings we really ate up the miles.

We had no time to lose. It was getting late for river travel. Soon snow melt would be running down the creeks into the river, cracks would open and slush would replace the hard snow. We saw one such place, spotting it long before we reached it, warned by the fog rising like white smoke at the mouth of a small creek. It forced us into a hard detour for half a mile through brush and timber.

The clear bright days wore on as we put the wilderness miles behind us. Evenings by the open fire, when Syd was asleep, Joyce and I talked of all the things we would do in the summer ahead, the places we'd see, the families and friends we'd visit. We had dreamed of all this for almost a year. Now it was coming closer to reality with each day of sled travel.

A sudden drop in temperature sent the thermometer plunging to forty-five below overnight and kept it there for three days. The dogs didn't mind, but the cold meant being very careful of Syd and stopping frequently to build a small fire and warm up with a pot of tea.

Only once did we meet another dog team. It was driven by two young Indian boys who were hauling a load of caribou meat from a kill made up in the mountains.

Not far above the roadhouse at Pelly Crossing, forty miles from Fort Selkirk, we came to the camp of Van Bibber, a famous hunting guide. His family welcomed us to a full dinner table and for the first time in two years we heard news of the outside world. Fur prices were high, the guide said, which delighted us. Then he added something we could not comprehend, about people in the cities going broke because of a stock market crash the fall before. We had no inkling then of what had happened in the autumn of 1929, and of the Great Depression that now held Canada and the United States in its grip.

But gold, Van Bibber told us, was still selling at twenty dollars an ounce. The eternal treasure had not suffered from the slump.

We reached the Pelly Crossing roadhouse on the fourteenth day after leaving Frances Lake. This was known as Schaffer's roadhouse, now operated by his widow, a big and capable woman who had managed the place alone since her husband died on a trip downriver to Fort Selkirk to get mail late in the fall. She cooked wonderful meals, kept a clean and warm hostelry, hunted most of her own moose and caribou meat, cursed like a dog musher, and was known and respected by everyone in the region.

The winter stage between Whitehorse and Dawson City consisted of a big tractor pulling two or three sleds behind it. One of these would be loaded with mail, and for a fare of $150 you could sit on the mail sacks and ride the "stage." It was a cold business, but there was no other form of transportation except dogsled. Each night the stage stopped at a roadhouse, running the tractor and loads into a barn while the travelers found accommodations inside. Schaffer's was about at the halfway point, where the winter road crossed the Pelly.

We had pulled in in early afternoon, and found good lodgings. We also learned that the stage from Dawson to Whitehorse, the way we were headed, was due in that evening. It would be bringing several passengers and Joyce and I reached a decision quickly. She and Syd would go on to Whitehorse by the stage. It would be fast, she would have the other passengers for company, and it would allow her and the boy the comforts of a roadhouse every night. From Whitehorse they would take the next train out to Skagway and then go on to Vancouver on the first steamship available. I'd catch up with them there. First I'd finish the sled trip to Whitehorse and trade our furs and sell our gold there.

This was an arrangement that meant safety and comfort for the family, less work for me on the trail, and time saved.

It would have been shorter and faster for me to leave the rivers here and follow the stage road, but I knew that at this time of year there would be too many miles bare of snow. I'd have to keep to the river ice, forty more miles down to Fort Selkirk, then up the Yukon, past Carmacks to Whitehorse.

The stage came roaring in as darkness fell. I saw my family off the next morning and then mushed the dogs downstream toward Fort Selkirk.

There, somewhat to my surprise, I found mail waiting for me, and there I also found a telegraph station and was able to send a cable off to my parents in England to let them know we were on our way.

There too I slept in a bed for the first time in two years. And with Bill Schoffield, a local trader, I enjoyed the first hot rum I had tasted in that same period of time. Need I say it tasted great?

I hit the trail at the first streaks of dawn the next morning, under crystal-clear skies with the temperature holding around forty below. The sled load was lightened now, with Joyce and Syd no longer riding, and there was a hard trail broken up the Yukon. The dogs fairly leaped ahead, and I was forced to ride the toboggan many times that day. They set a pace too fast for me to jog behind them.

It was just getting dark when I saw the lights of cabins upriver and heard the barking of dogs, and we pulled into the little settlement of Minto, fifty-eight miles from Selkirk. That was a record day for me, the longest run I had ever made with a dog team between daylight and dark.

To my astonishment, I was expected, and greeted by name the minute I halted my team. The Yukon telegraph line, a single wire stretching across the mountains and rivers from Hazelton in central British Columbia through Whitehorse and down the Yukon to Dawson City, passed through all of these river settlements, and at each one the operator relayed the day's news. It was news that I had arrived at

Selkirk and left, and the people at Minto were expecting me, although not until the next day. If I had not shown up then a search party would have gone out to learn why.

I was on the homestretch now, with two hundred and fifty miles to go from Selkirk to Whitehorse. There'd be frequent roadhouses, at Carmacks, Big Salmon, Yukon Crossing, and Little River.

The days went by quickly, but a thaw set in, the temperature suddenly warming to forty above during the day. Afternoon sled travel became impossible. The crust would no longer hold the dogs. We camped at noon and mushed out at night as soon as falling temperatures hardened the surface of the snow. Even on cloudy nights the snow reflected enough light for travel, and I knew I could trust Rogue not to lead the team onto unsafe ice. He seemed to have a sixth sense in his paws that warned him of danger ahead of time.

Two hours after breaking camp in the darkness, on what I figured was our last day, we struck the foot of Lake Lebarge. The lake is about twenty-eight miles long, and much of the snow had melted off now, leaving glare ice, slick and smooth, on which the dogs could find no footing. The toboggan slid this way and that, and I strained to hold it on course.

Around midnight the clouds cleared away, and we pulled ashore to make tea and rest for an hour.

The lake had ice about five feet thick, but the water was rising fast under it, and thundering booms broke the silence, rumbling across the ice like muffled drums. It was the same sound we had heard at breakup time on Frances Lake, and once I was ashore it seemed all the louder.

When I pulled onto the lake again I drove the dogs out a half mile from shore to avoid any danger of thin ice, knowing that lakes thaw first along the beach. The groaning and booming under our feet was an eerie thing, and it stirred a vague sense of danger in me. But the dogs kept their steady pace, tails held high. It was just the weariness and the loneliness of traveling the snows alone the last few days, I told myself.

The night was one of rare beauty, with a pale moon casting its ghostly light over the shore, where the trees stood freighted with snow. The shadows of the dogs and the sled raced beside us as we toiled ahead, and the hickory boards of the toboggan made a soothing, rustling sound as they swished over the snow and the patches of clear ice.

I was very tired and the stillness of the night and the song of the sled were lulling me into drowsiness. Then Rogue stopped in his tracks, so suddenly that the rest of the team piled up on top of one another in a tangle of harness. My drowsiness was gone in an instant. I knew my lead dog had a good reason for what he had done.

I went ahead to untangle the snarling team and straighten them out in their traces, and as they quieted I thought I heard the sound of water, like small waves lapping on a beach. I hushed the dogs to complete silence and listened intently. The sound was unmistakable. It was water, lapping against the ice just ahead. I broke into a cold sweat, aware of the great danger I was in. I could see a bank of mist lying over the lake where the open water lay.

I scouted forward very cautiously, until the sound of waves was clear and strong, and I knew what had happened. The ice in the river above the head of the lake had broken, and running water was now lapping against the rotting ice of the lake itself.

In all my years in the Yukon I had had no closer call than that. I had been too near to sleep to sense the danger and halt the dogs in time. Had Rogue led the team into that danger zone and gone through, he almost certainly would have taken the others and the sled with him and I would have followed. The current under the ice would have swept everything with it instantly, too. Dogs and sled and man might have been found on some sandbar when summer came, along with the pokes of gold, or the lake might have kept forever the secret of what had happened.

I wasn't drowsy now. I turned the dogs back on their own trail, mushed them for half an hour, and turned to the shore. There was good ice along the narrow beach, and we fought through tangles of willow and down timber onto higher ground. Daylight was only an hour or two away, and I decided to make camp and rest a few hours.

I fed the dogs their ration of dried whitefish, made a fire, and thawed a fat moose steak. I did not bother with the tent. Since leaving Fort Selkirk, with no family to shelter, I had been sleeping in my bag on top of the load on the toboggan, using the tent for a mattress. I ate, slid into the welcome warmth of the bag, and was instantly asleep.

I awoke to find the morning well along. The sky was cloudy, the temperature around forty above. I had thirty very tough miles ahead to Whitehorse.

The river ice was gone and I was several miles from the winter tractor road, which, even if I reached it, would have long stretches of bare ground. There was nothing for it but to fight my way through timber and underbrush, breaking trail in the deep and slushy snow, helping the dogs around trees and thickets and along steep hillsides.

It was slow and tiring work. I was soaked to the skin quickly, from the wet snow underfoot and also from the small avalanches that fell on me from the tree branches as I clawed through. The dogs became tired and irritable, piling up on uneven ground, nipping at the one ahead if he held back. We traveled by daylight to see our way and at dusk I made camp in a stand of spruce.

I put in a restless night, and awoke to find the sky clear and the sun high. I must have been bone-tired to be caught in my bag in that fashion, I chided myself.

I was sure we were only a few miles from Whitehorse now and I made up my mind that I did not want another night on the trail. I had come more than six hundred miles since leaving Frances Lake three weeks before. I was sure that Joyce and Syd had caught a train out to Skagway. By now they were probably aboard ship, on the way down the coast to Vancouver, or already there. It was time to end this winter odyssey.

I broke trail for hours, helping the dogs through the soft and slushy snow. Just before dark I stopped for a rest and tea, confident that we must be close to town. A covey of ptarmigan flew up and lit on the snow a hundred feet ahead. I decapitated one with the rifle, and made a fire, splitting the bird and skewering it on a forked willow to broil. The dogs rested while I ate and drank tea. Dusk fell suddenly and we hit out again.

Suddenly we came out on a well-used trail where the travel was easy. The team perked up, and in another two or three miles the trail ran into the winter road. The hardships were behind us now. I could even put that open water at the head of Lebarge out of my mind.

Lights shone in the darkness ahead. We passed the first outlying cabins, and tied dogs set up a drawn-out, haunting chorus, close akin to the howling of a wolf pack.

We struck the ruts of tractors and truck tires, where Whitehorse hauled its water from a creek two miles out of town. I halted my team, tied sleighbells to the top of each harness. We'd end the trip in style.

There must have been two hundred sled dogs in White-horse and the musical jinglejangle of those bells set them howling in unison. It was a grand and suitable announce-ment of our arrival.

We drove up in front of the Whitehorse Inn, with its wide double doors and lights burning in the lobby. It stood as the symbol of everything I had dreamed about for months. George King, the handsome and very pleasant Japanese who owned the place, stood on the porch at the top of a flight of wide snow-covered steps, waving a welcome.

I ignored the hitching posts at the foot of those steps.

"Mush, you sons-of-bitches!" I shouted happily to the dogs, "Up there, Rogue! Mush!"

King threw the double doors wide open and the team piled up the snow-covered stairs. They were across the lobby and halfway back to the kitchens when I halted them with a sharp "Whoa!" The toboggan came to rest in front of the roaring fire in the lobby fireplace.

King helped me unharness the dogs and took them out through the back door to kennels. I threw off my parka and sprawled spread-eagled in a big leather armchair. George shoved a glass of hot buttered rum into my hand, reported that Joyce and Syd had taken a train to the coast three days before, and told me some of the men in town had laid plans to go down to Lake Lebarge and look for me if I did not show up by noon the next day.

I downed the buttered rum and headed for bed. The man from Frances Lake was out!

I slept and partied for three days. Friends came into the lobby and unpacked some of my furs and shook them out, testing the fineness of the silky marten and mink skins. They untied a poke of the gold, weighing the nuggets in the palms of their hands, estimating the worth. Thieving was practically unknown in the Yukon before the Second World War. Sometimes there was a killing, but there was usually a reason for killing a man—there was no excuse for theft.

I am confident that I had not lost a single nugget when, three days later, I took the gold across the street to Jim Wheeler at the Canadian Bank of Commerce. He emptied the pokes into the pan on one side of the huge gold scales on the counter, adding brass weights into the other pan until the scale balanced. He then credited my account with close to $17,000! A fortune. In purchasing power it would be equal to about eight times that amount today—more than $135,000.

I took the rest of my furs over to the Taylor & Drury Store and cashed them in, then went over to the White Pass and Yukon Route depot where I bought a C.P.R. deluxe passage for the family to England. "Mac" McLaughlin, who had been agent for the White Pass since it was built at the time of the Dawson Stampede, told me mine was the longest ticket he had ever sold. I doubt he had ever served a happier customer, either.

George King had promised to look after my dogs until I returned. We planned to return over next year's late spring snow to our gold diggings at the Half-Moon.

This vacation was going to be the grandest vacation any family ever had, and we had plenty to come back to. The hard work. The satisfaction of recovering gold from our own discovery. The glory and peacefulness of the wilderness.

The high mountains with their ever-changing beauty. The fishing, the hunting, the great inner feeling of independence and freedom and accomplishment without any outsider's help. We knew the wild and beautiful and lonely North we both loved would be there to welcome us home.

This was the North—the good life.

EPILOG

I am not eager to set down the final chapter of this story, for it does not have a happy ending. But I realize readers will want to know what came after—and are entitled to be told.

Our second son, Tony, was born in Vancouver shortly after we got back from England in 1930.

On the way, in New York, I was asked by a Boston mining company to visit them. Gold was the one rock-firm commodity in those black years at the start of the Depression, and I was "the Man from Eldorado," who had come out with a healthy stake. I was regarded as an expert at finding the precious stuff.

I was offered a contract with highly favorable terms, to examine mining properties in Yukon Territory for this company. That was the first of a series of similar well-paid jobs, and I continued working as a field scout for mining companies until World War II began.

I checked gold mining properties and prospects all over northern British Columbia and the Yukon, and in some instances developed them into production. I reopened an underground placer mine on Lightning Creek in northern British Columbia and put a crew of four hundred men to work there. I made a new discovery on the Tahltan River above the Indian village referred to in the early chapters of the book, built seven miles of road to it, and installed a complete hydraulic plant with a crew of thirty Indians. I started the China Bar mine and operated the first bulldozers and carryalls to be used in British Columbia mining history. Then the war closed us down.

With the forced closing of gold mines I was ordered by the Canadian Federal Government at Ottawa to work as superintendent of an explosives plant north of Toronto, in charge of three thousand men. When I managed to get out of that job I went back to the North and ran twelve dog-team crews, surveying the route over the McKenzie Mountains for the Canol Pipeline. The last war years I spent as assistant superintendent for the Kansas City Bridge Company, helping build the airports of Whitehorse and Watson Lake, in the Yukon.

We managed only one year's stay at Frances Lake during those years. In 1936 we flew in a small plane, landing on the ice at the silver-lead claims on the East Arm, and flew out again the following April, after developing the claims for a full year.

In 1945 I flew by charter plane to Frances Lake and sold the Half-Moon to a mining company.

Joyce and I had twenty-four happy years together. Then something went wrong. Although she was with me during much of my work in the Yukon wilderness, and later in small mining towns and camps, there were, of necessity, long periods of time when I was away from her. During my war work she lived in Edmonton, helping the boys through high school. Later we made a home in Santa Barbara, California, and I took a job operating a large lime quarry on the Mojave Desert with a crew of thirty Mexican Americans.

Perhaps those times apart were too frequent and prolonged for a woman of her emotional makeup. In any event, she fell in love with another man, got a Nevada divorce, and married him. I was at the lime quarry when word came to me. I turned the job over to another, and quit. For a year I was in a state of shock—bewildered, distraught, and wretched.

Then I took another post, as associate engineer at the University of California, Santa Barbara, designing and overseeing construction of roads, walks, water systems, and drainage on the four-hundred-acre campus, on land as flat as a billiard table.

While there I met Jerry Walker, and in 1951, when I was fifty and Jerry forty-six, we were married. The lure of the North was still strong in me. I quit my job and in spring of 1952 we went north and built and operated a hunting and fishing lodge on the Alaska Highway near Muncho Lake, known as The Village Inn.

Joyce's husband was killed in a private plane crash in 1956, and she died of cancer in the summer of 1972.

Syd married and has two children. He is now living in Las Vegas selling real estate. Tony graduated from Stanford as a civil engineer and is now a senior engineer with a large San Francisco firm. He married and lives very happily with his wife and two boys.

Jerry and I were a happy team until 1964. We then decided to sell out the Village, which we had taken twelve hardworking years to build from scratch, and return to California. Shortly before we were ready to leave she died in her sleep from a heart attack. Again I was plunged into depths of despair—and came south alone.

The years since have been lonely ones for me. I returned to Santa Barbara, where I am at present, mostly with my memories.

But they are magnificent memories.

I can close my eyes and still see the beauty of Frances Lake and the mountains around it. I remember the savage rapids in the canyons of the Liard and the Frances, the Christmas caribou that licked salt from my hand, the log cabins I built, my dogs and the soft whisper of a toboggan over snow. I remember the fun and ecstasy Joyce and I found by ourselves, in the solitude of the remote wilderness —the silence of the winter nights, the terrible cold of seventy-five below. I even remember and can laugh at the poling boat and the whipsaw and the hard trips under pack.

The North I came to from England at twenty-two was a land of untamed splendor. The mountains and the rivers, the summer heat and winter cold, the hard work and solitude taught me lessons I could have learned in no other school on earth. It fulfilled my every dream and transformed me from a green cheechako into a self-reliant woodsman, skilled in the things a man must know to survive by himself in a vast and harsh world.

That North still lives—bright as a nugget inside me.

Gardner Webb College Library